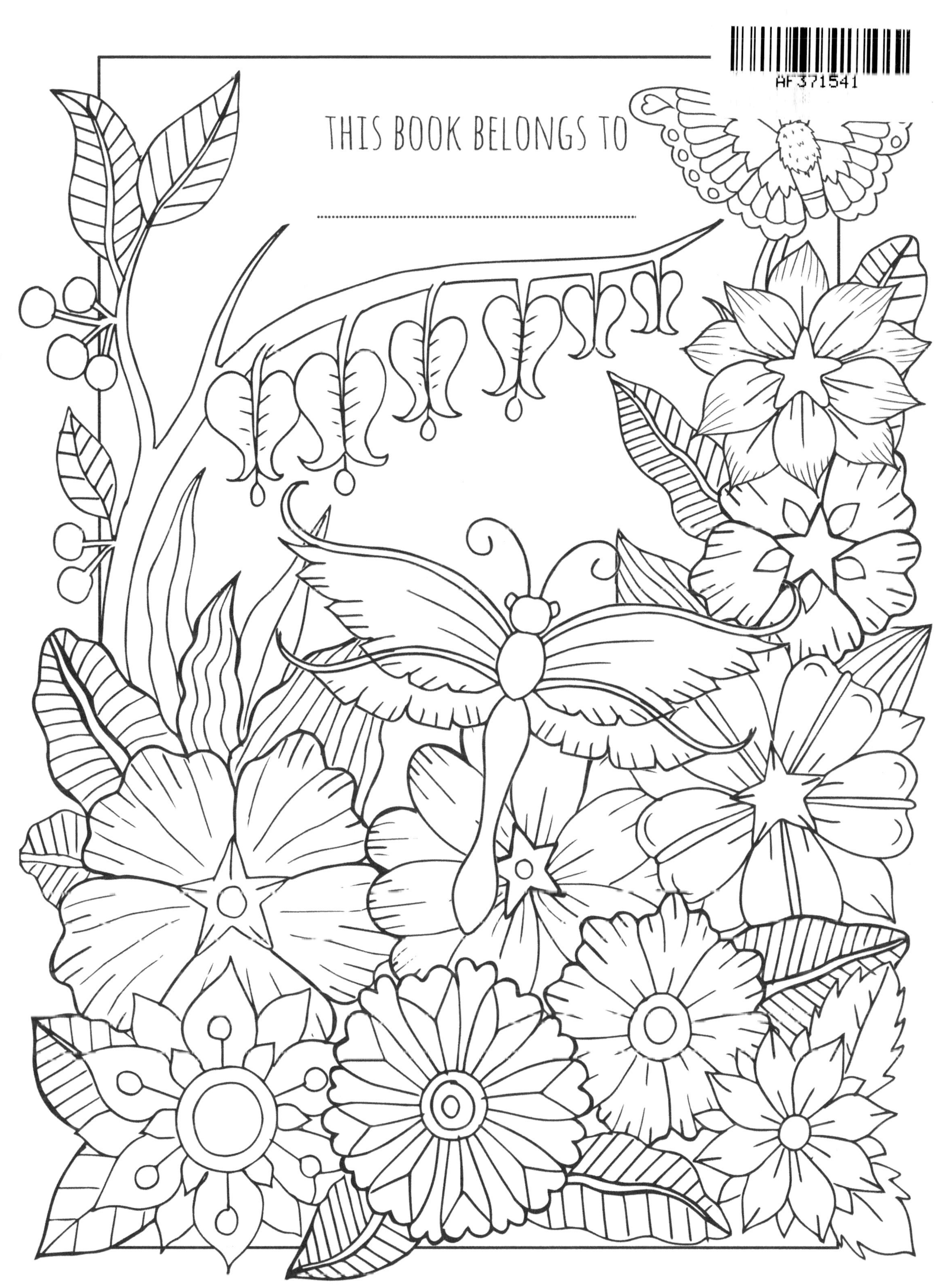
THIS BOOK BELONGS TO
AF371541

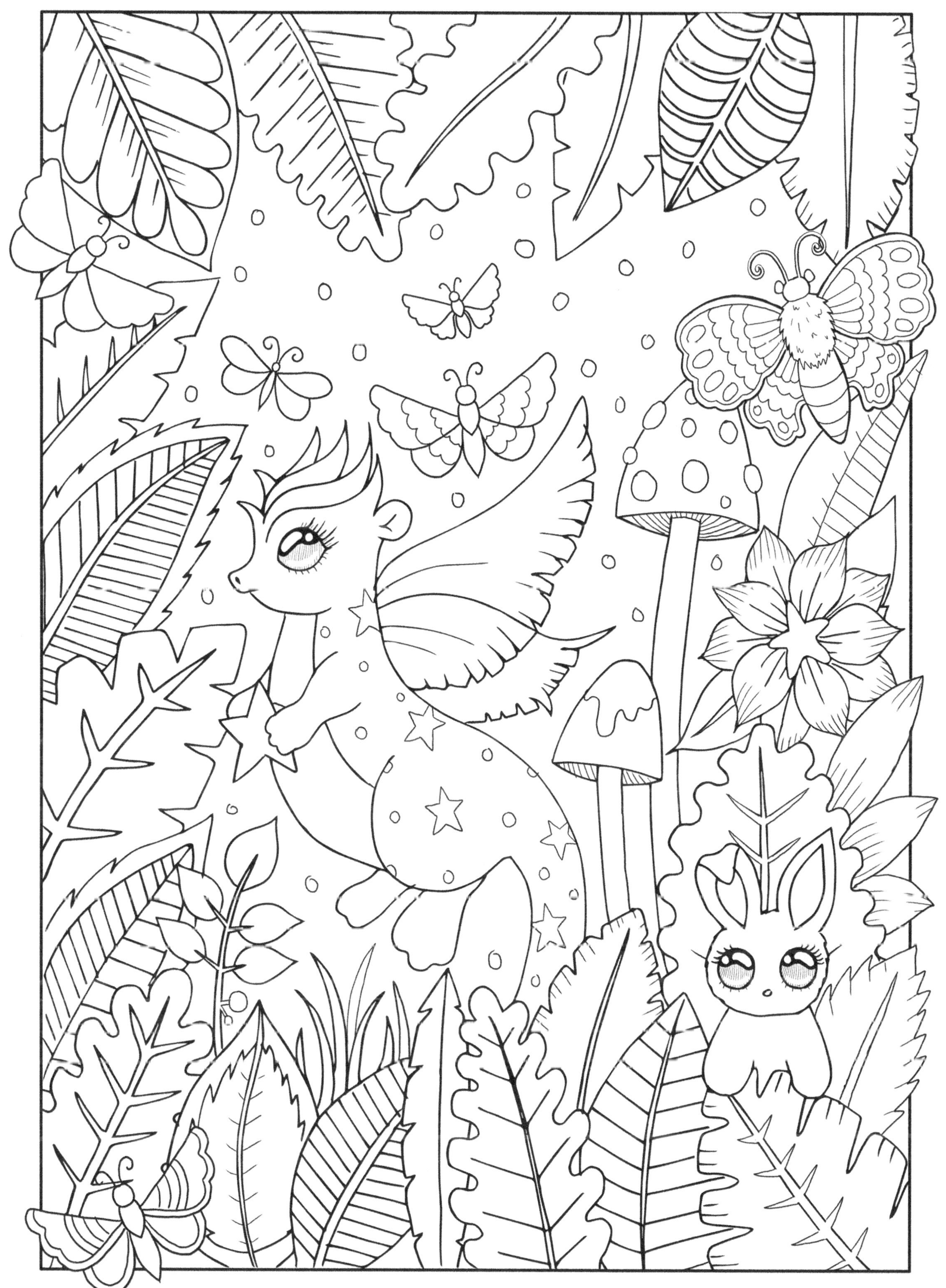

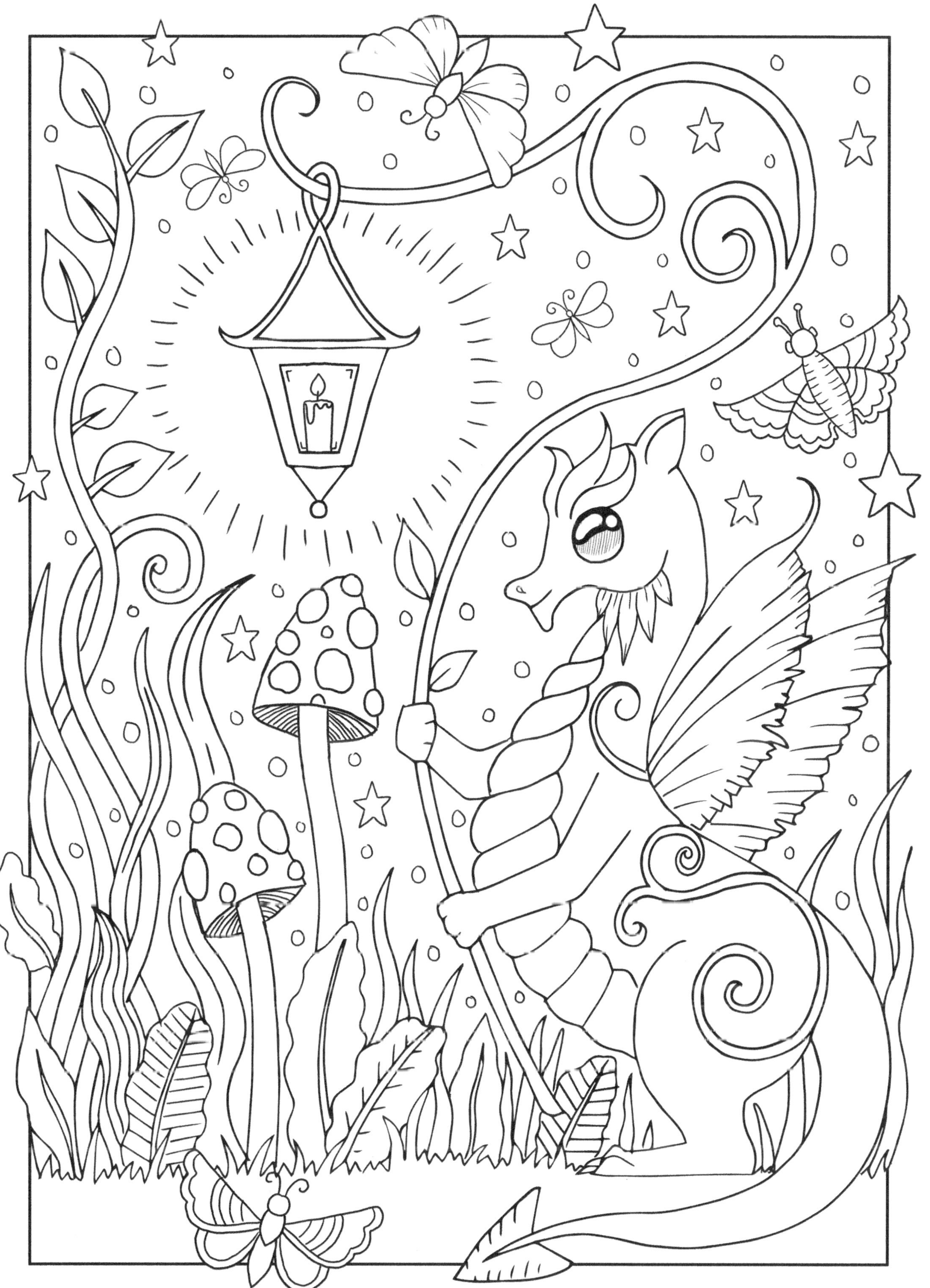

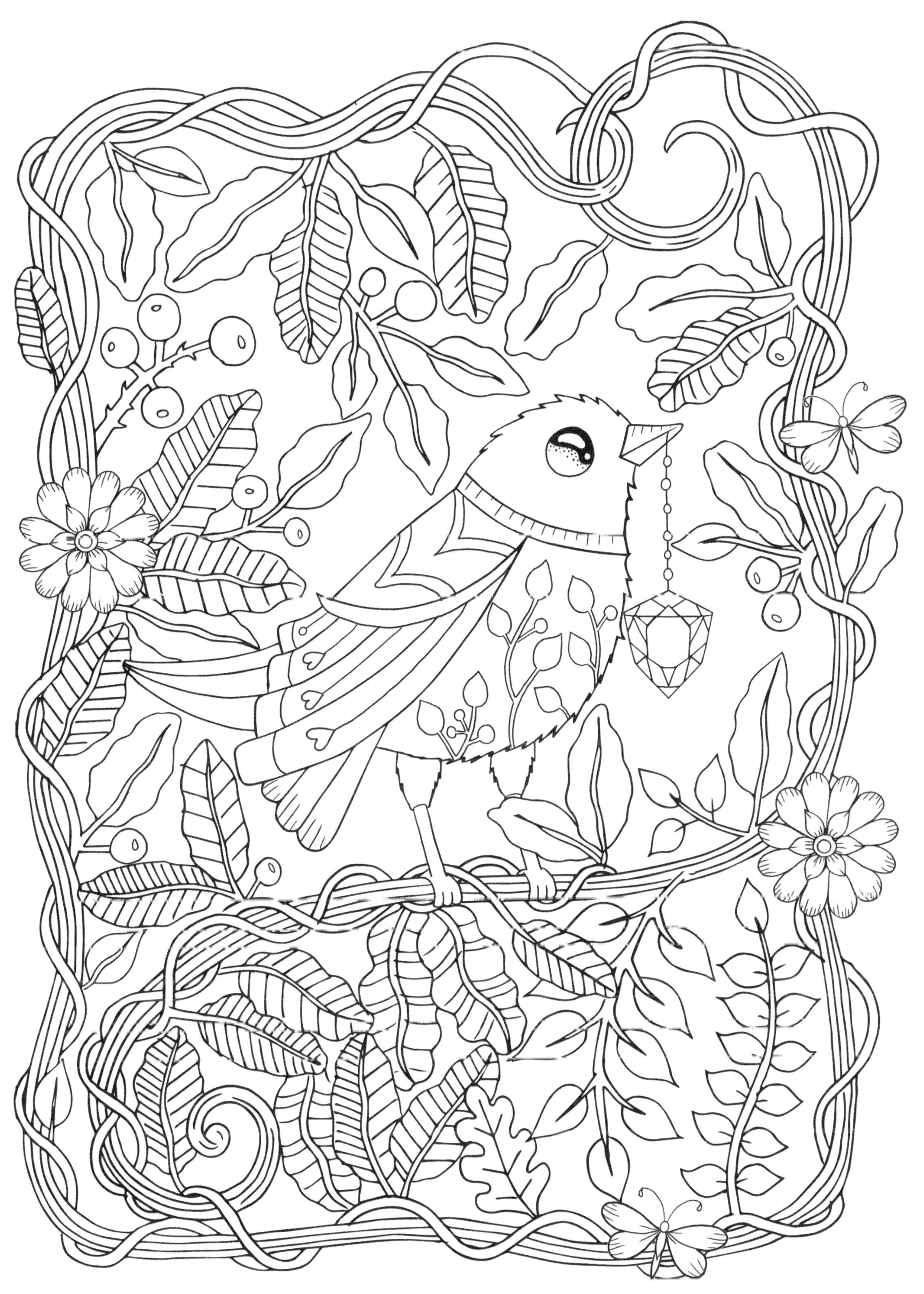

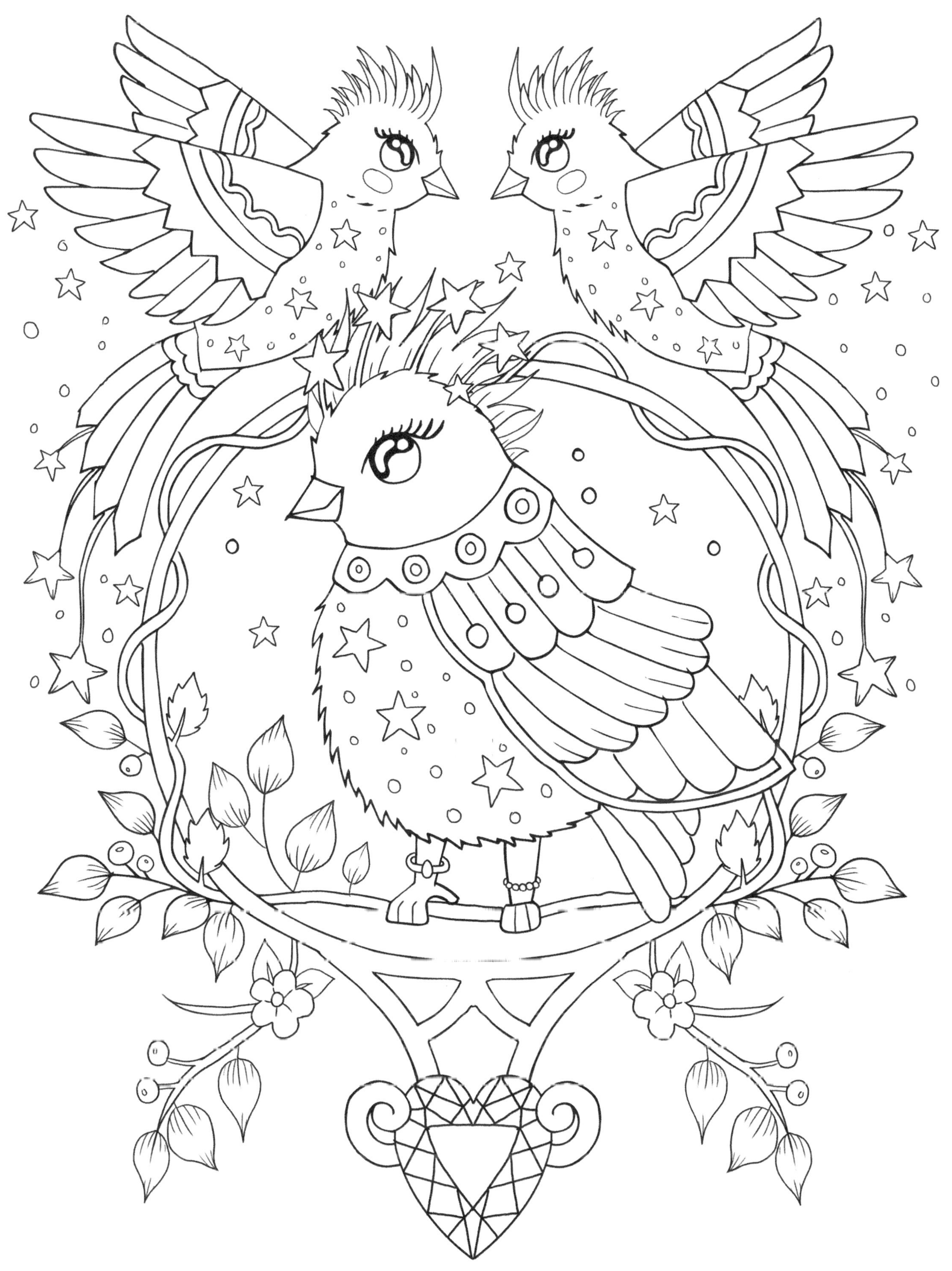

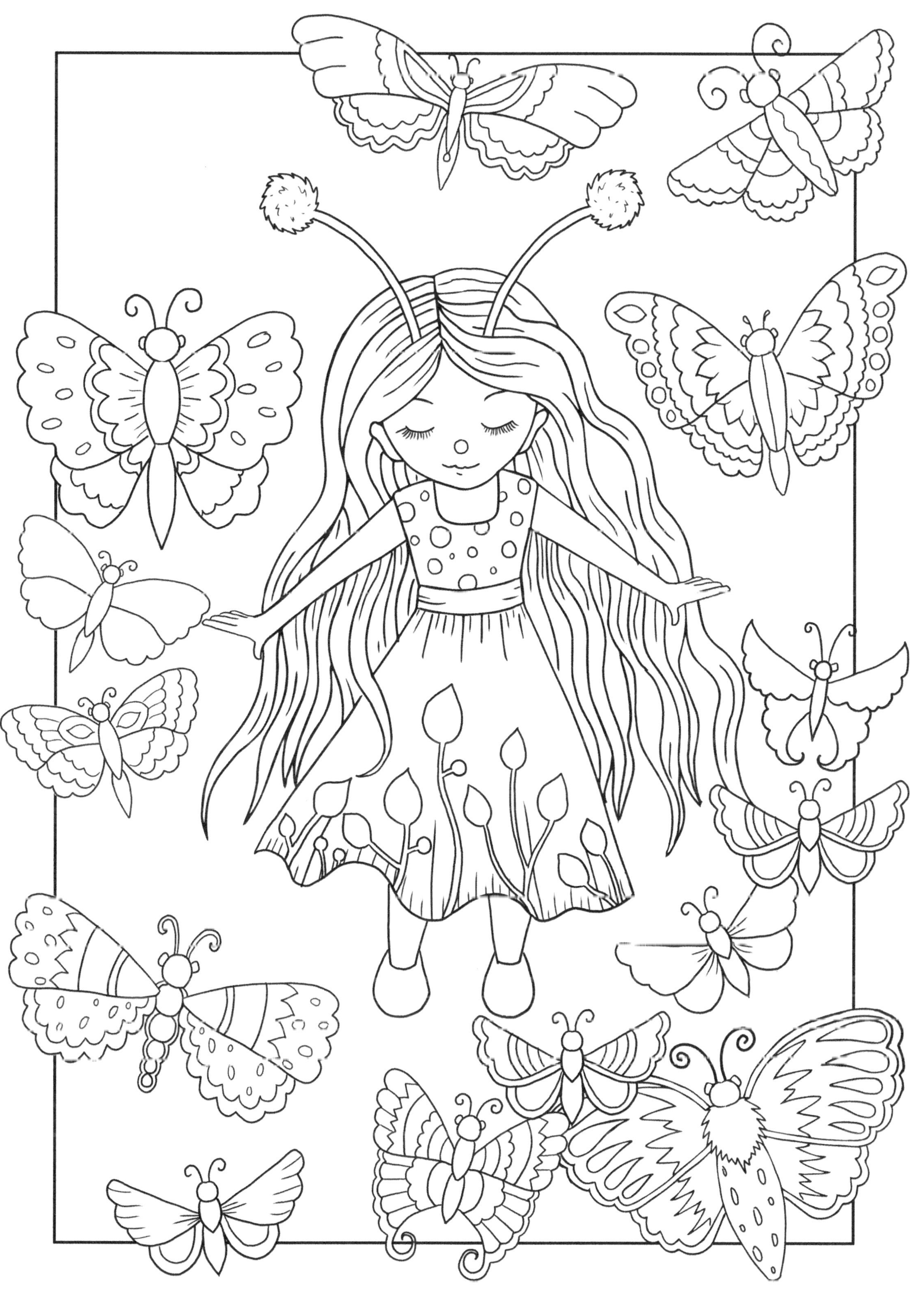

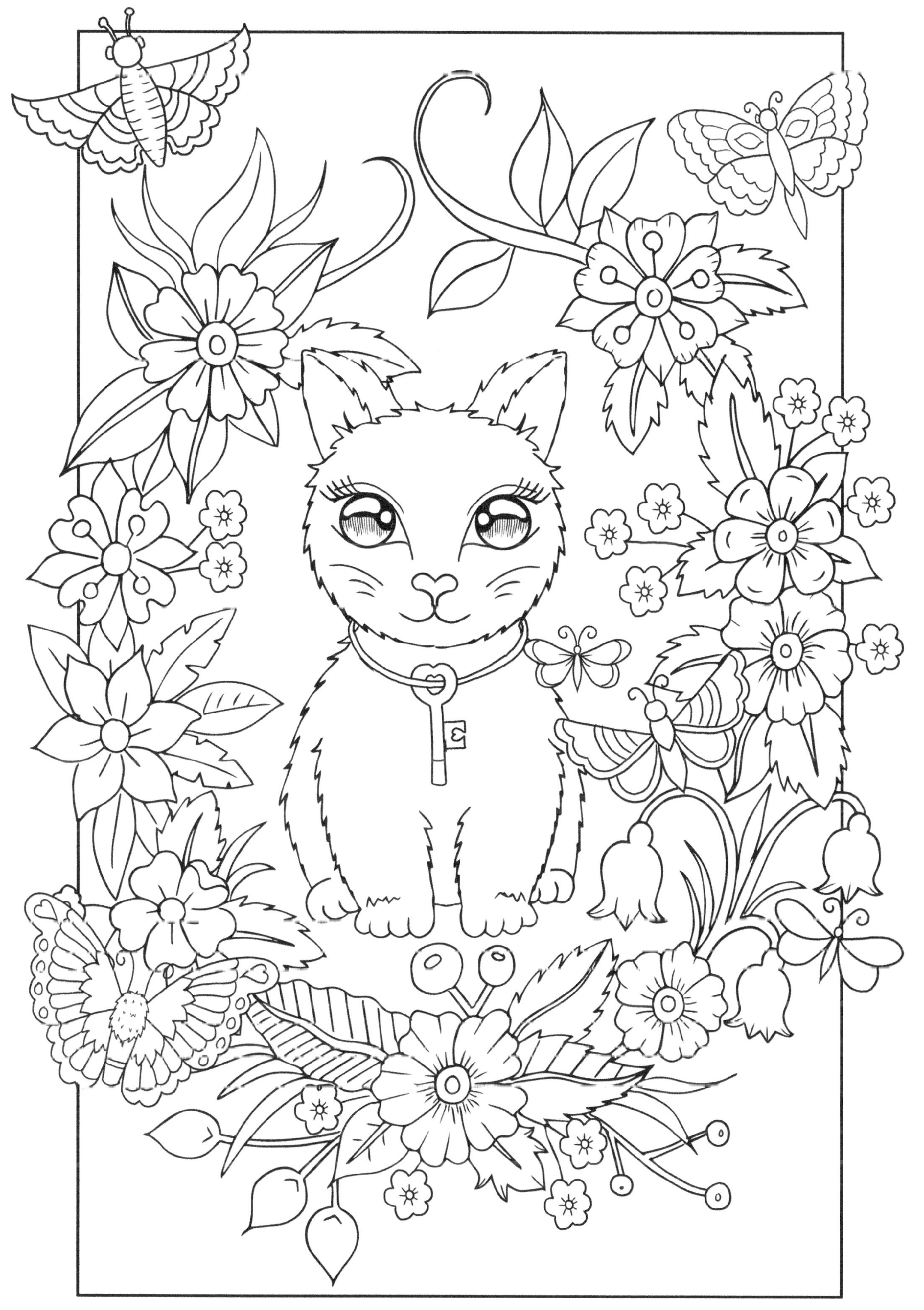

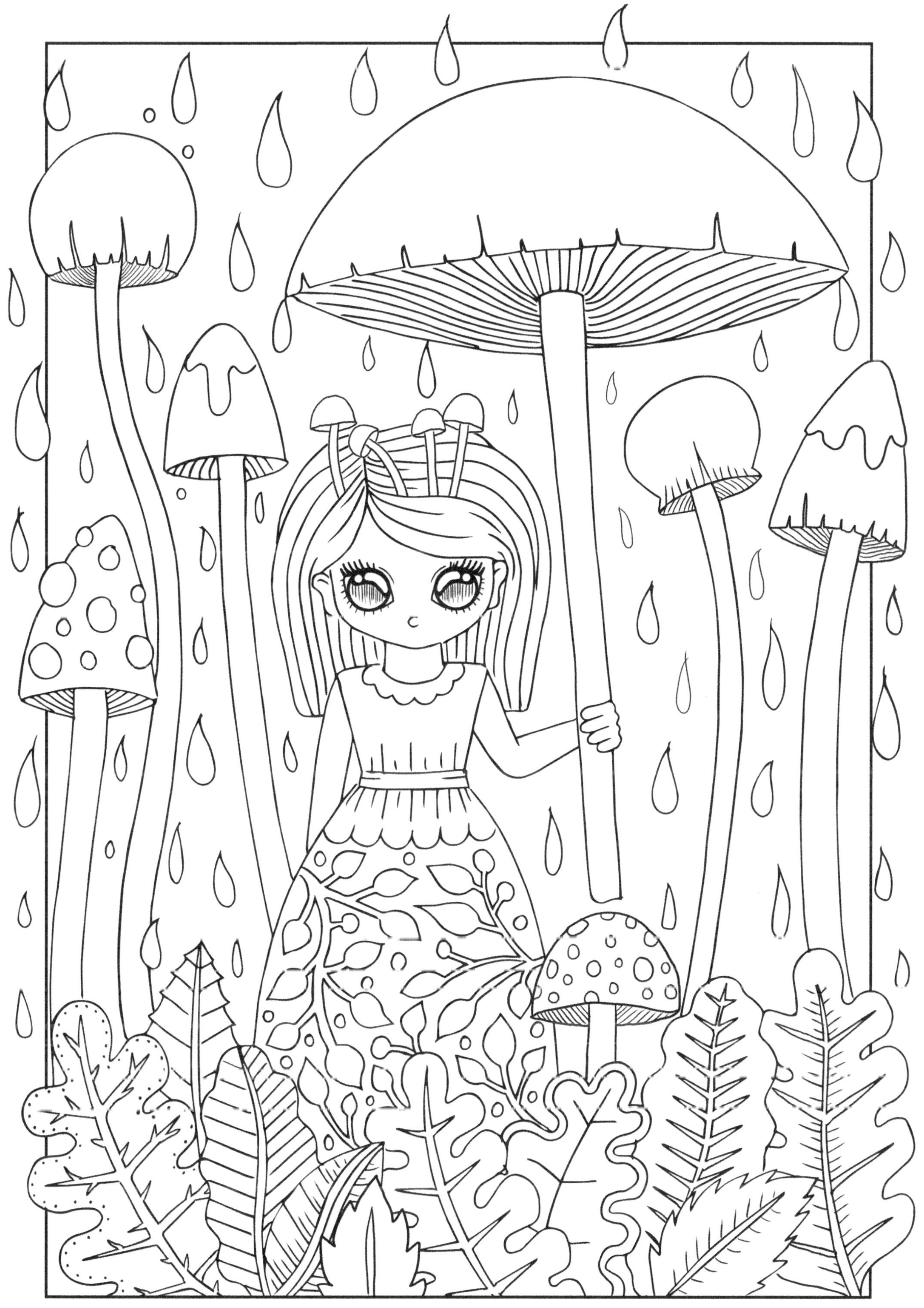

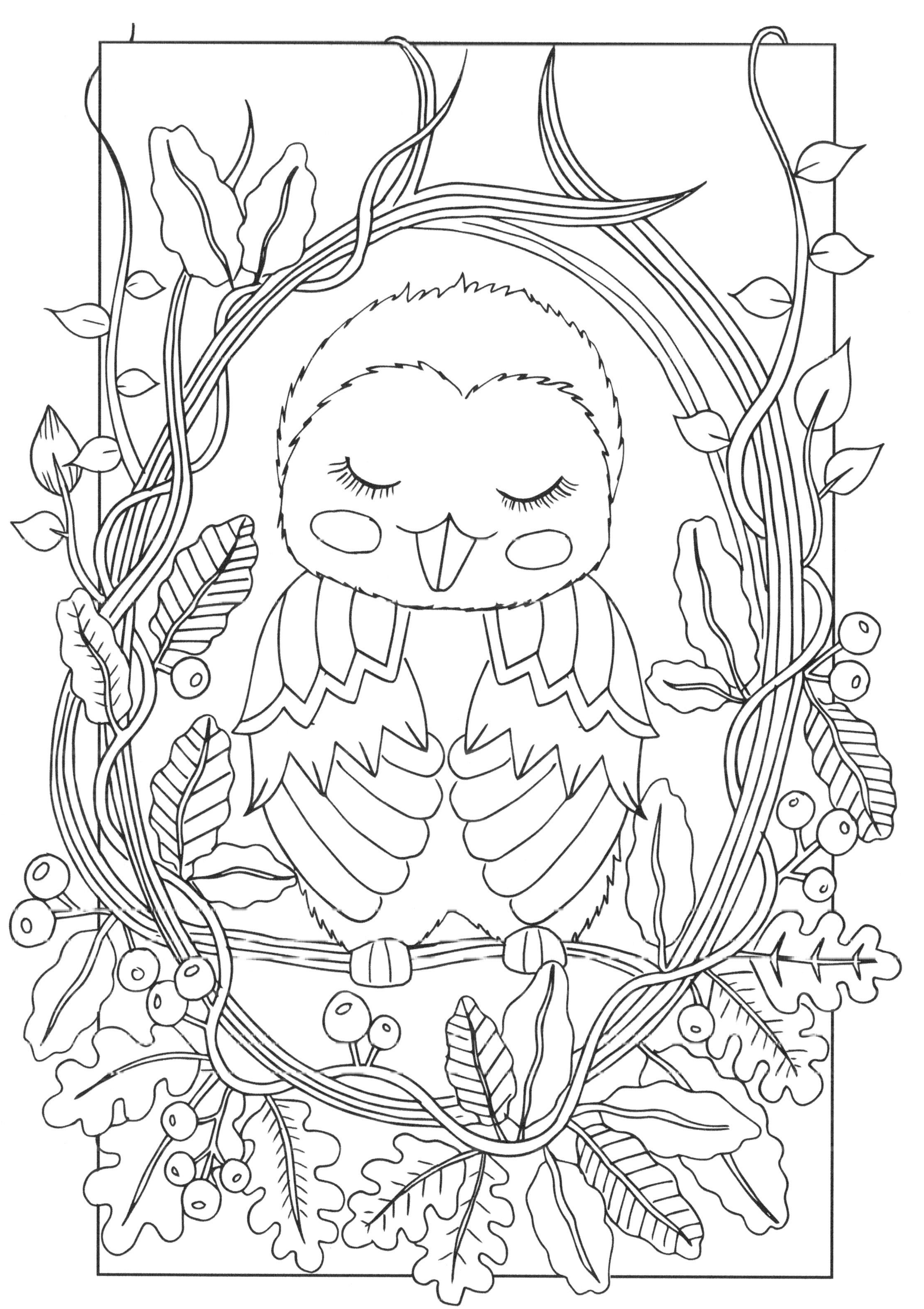

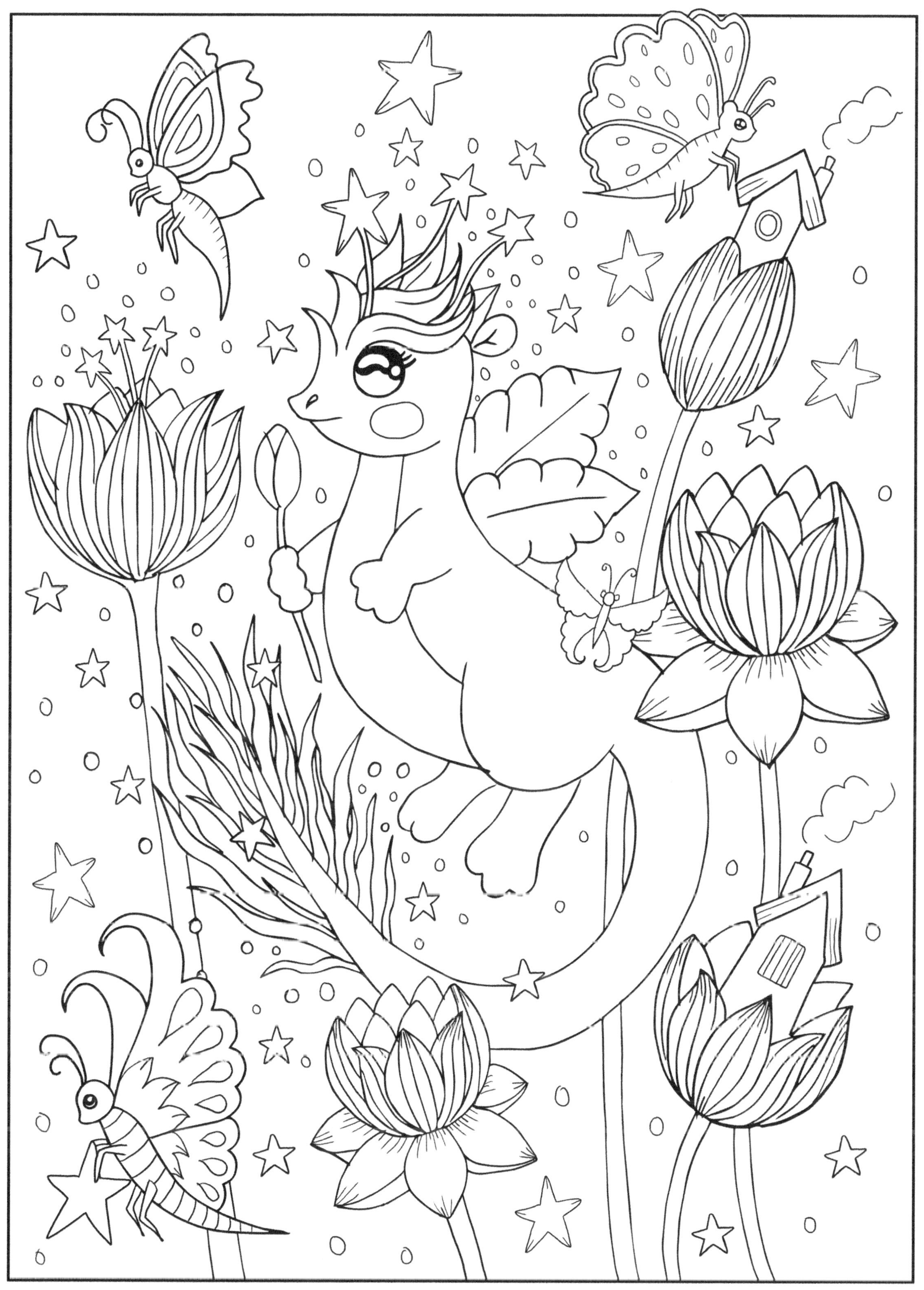

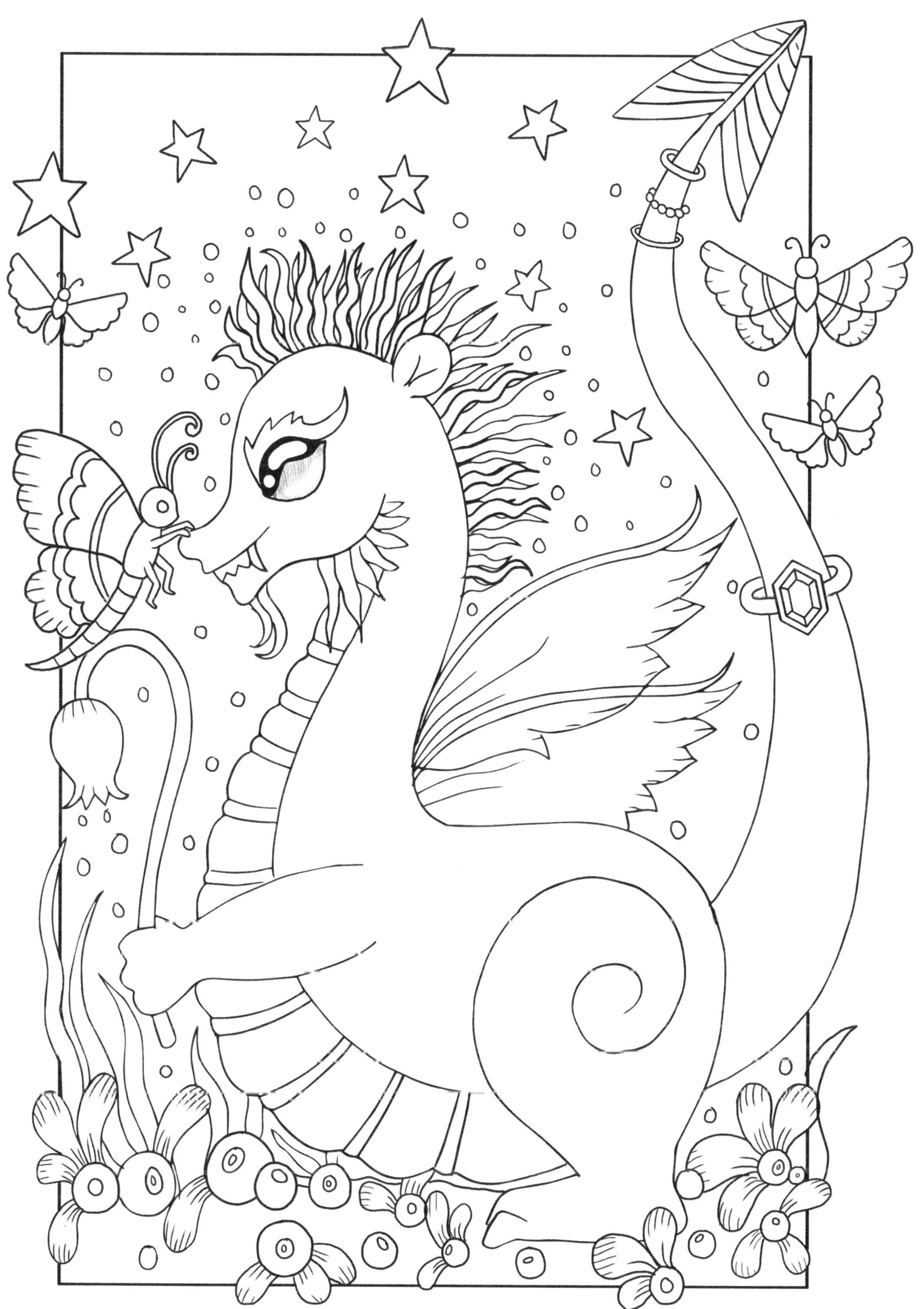

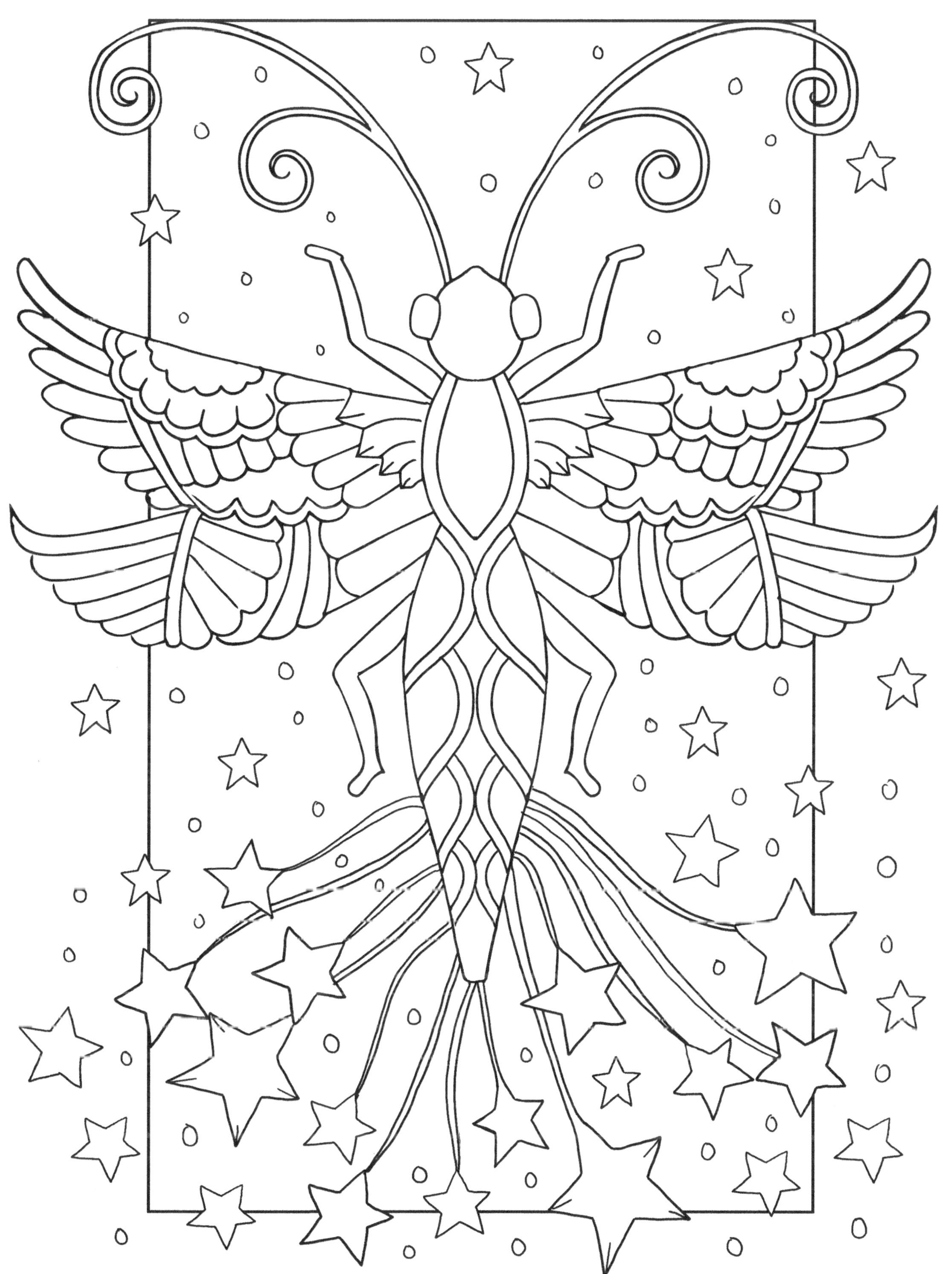

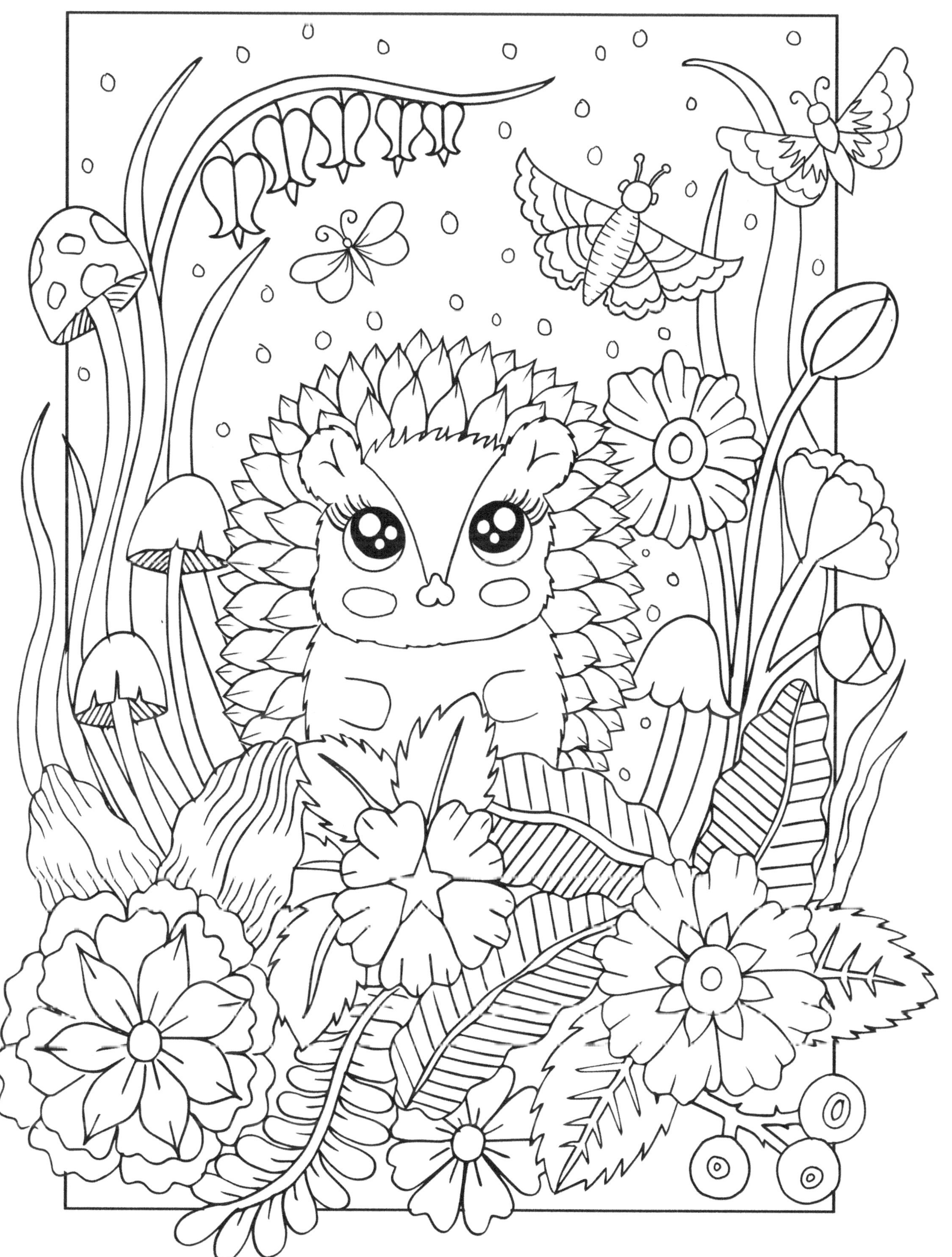

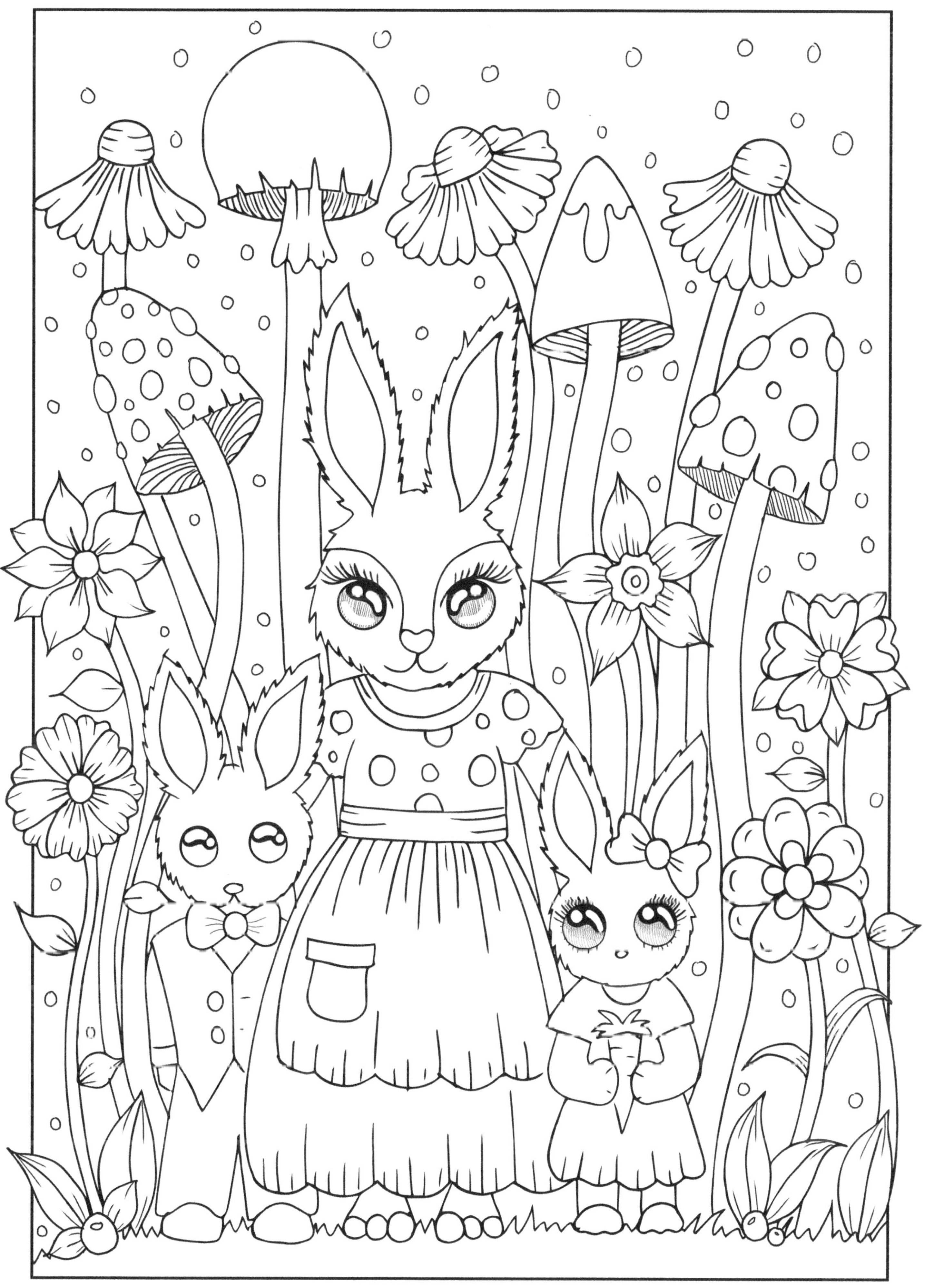

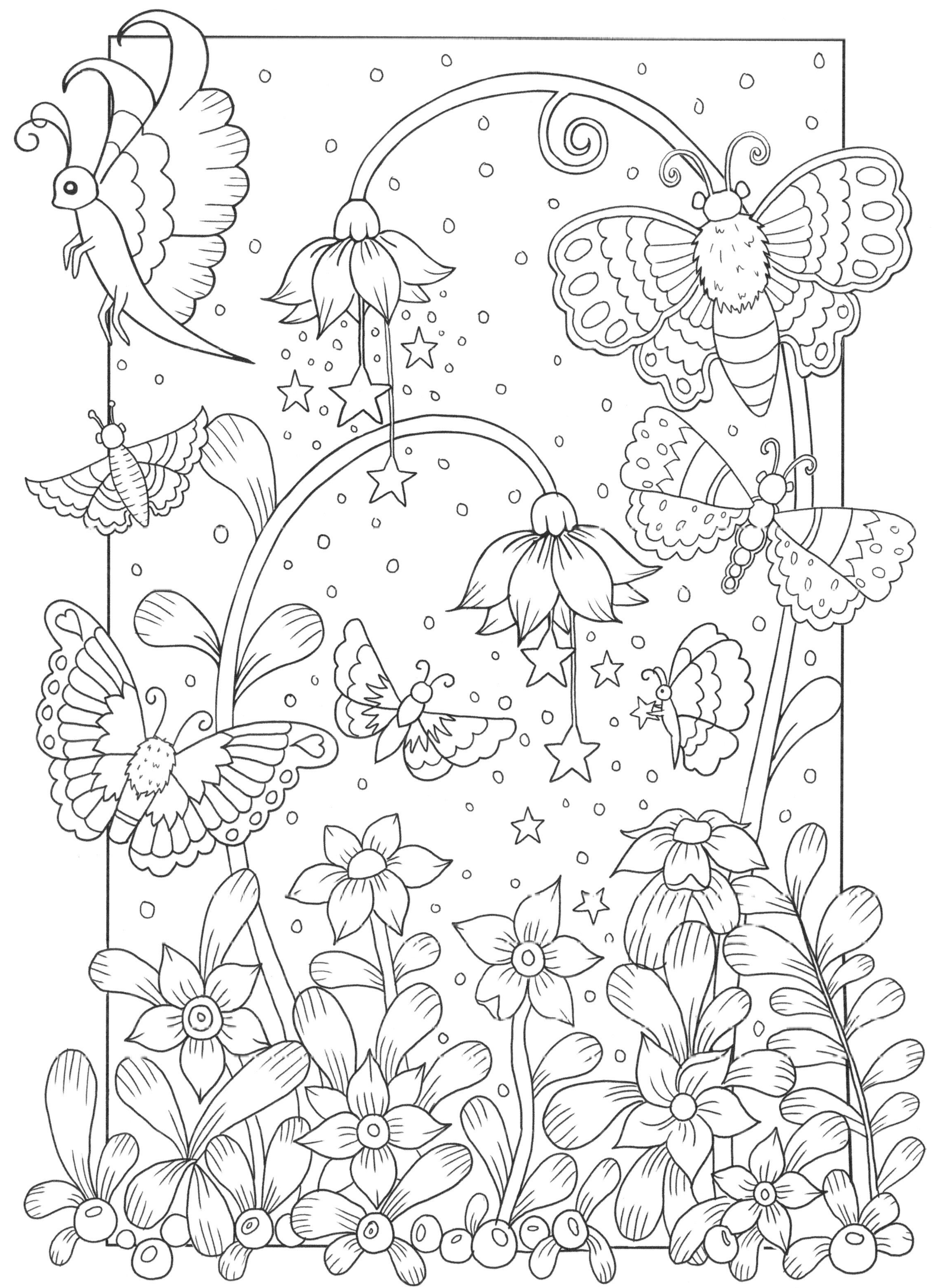

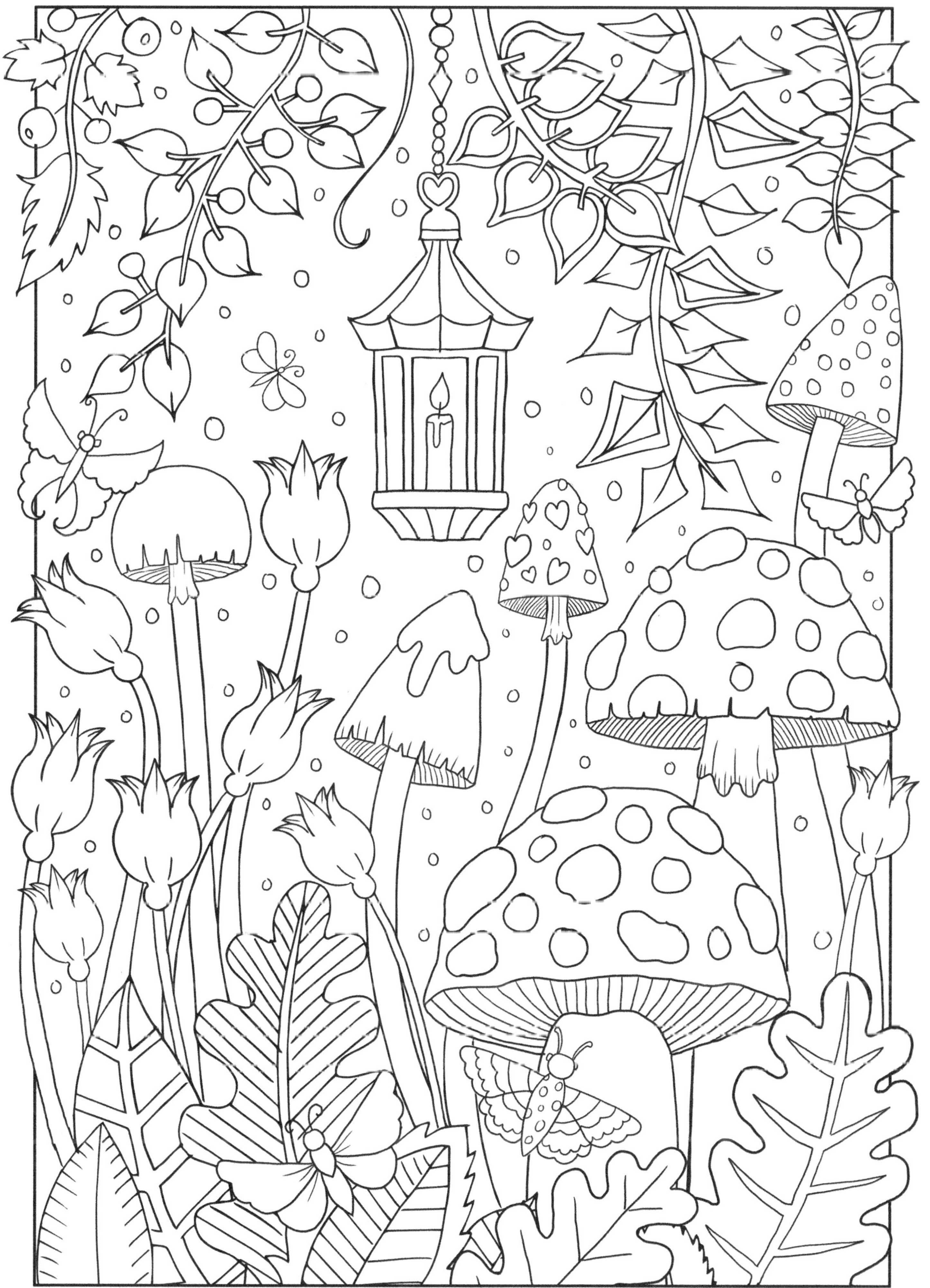

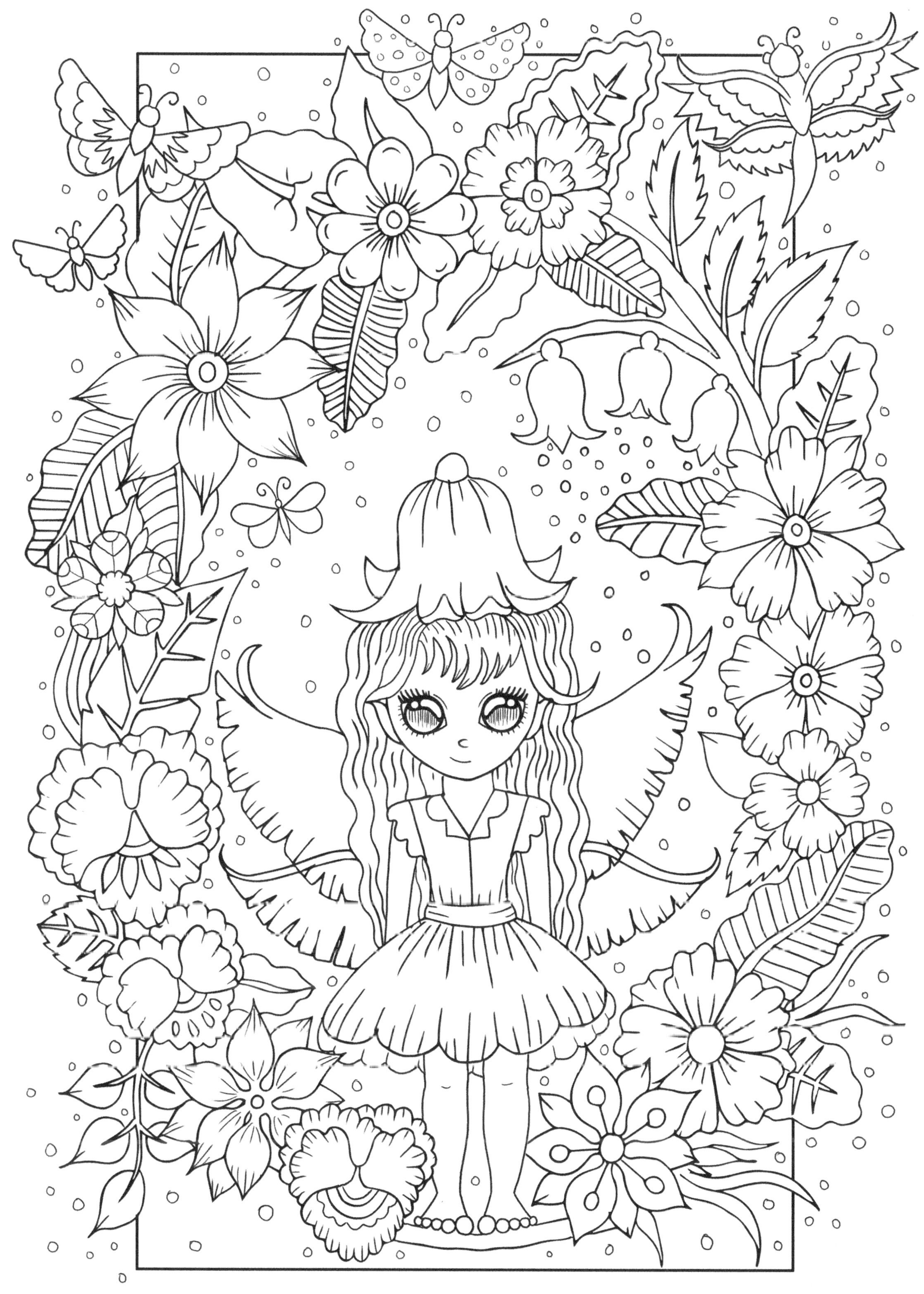

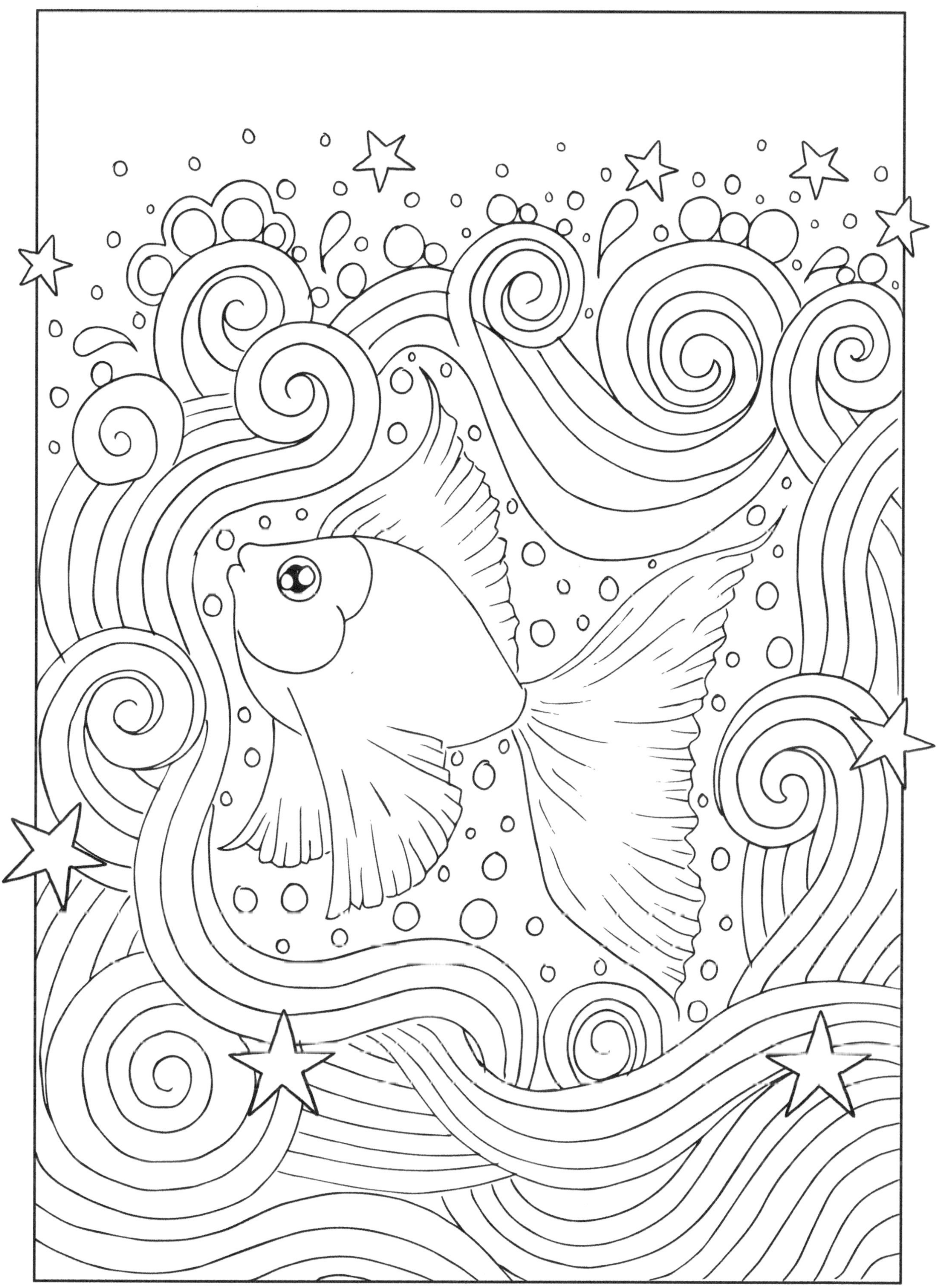

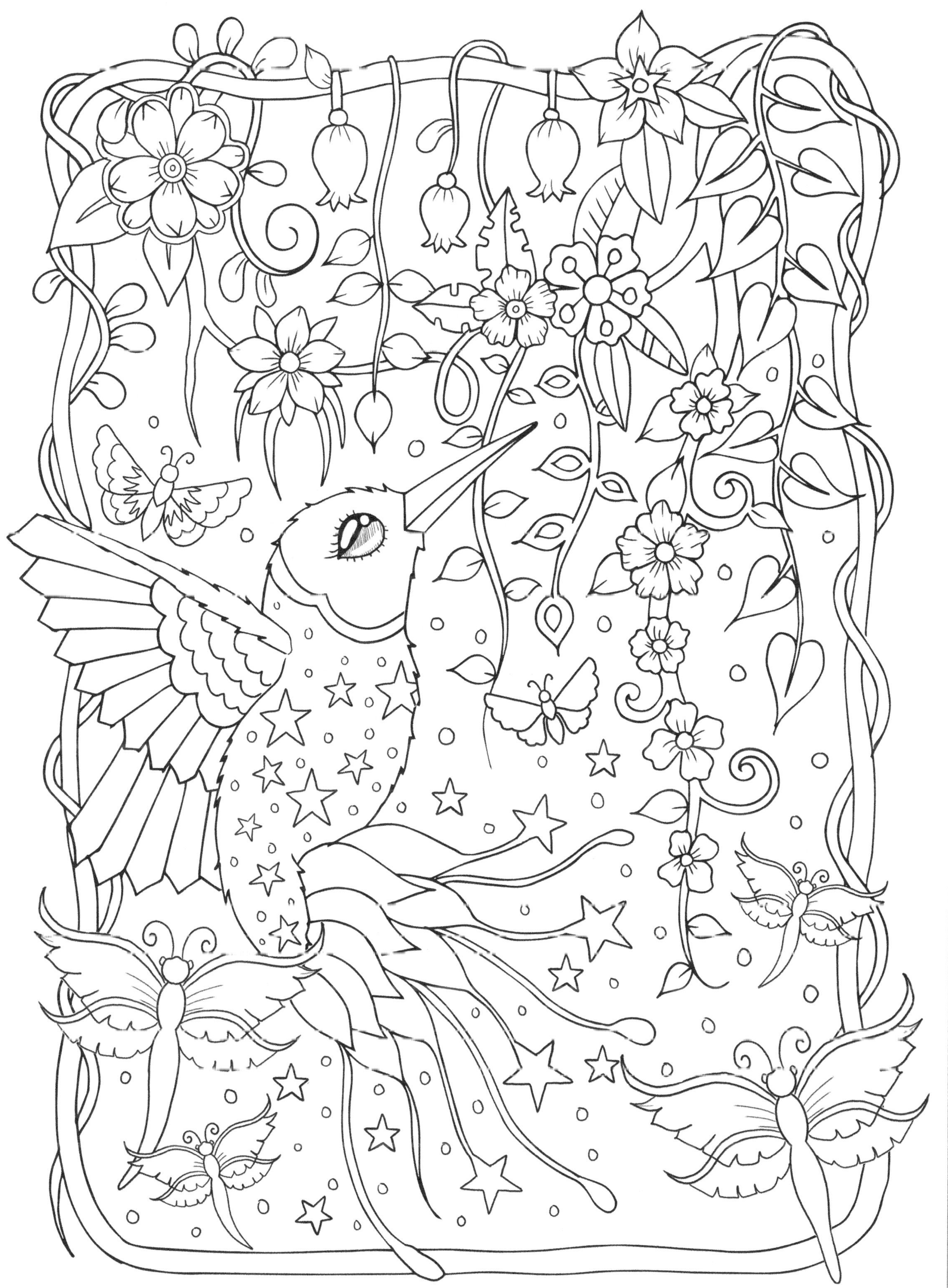

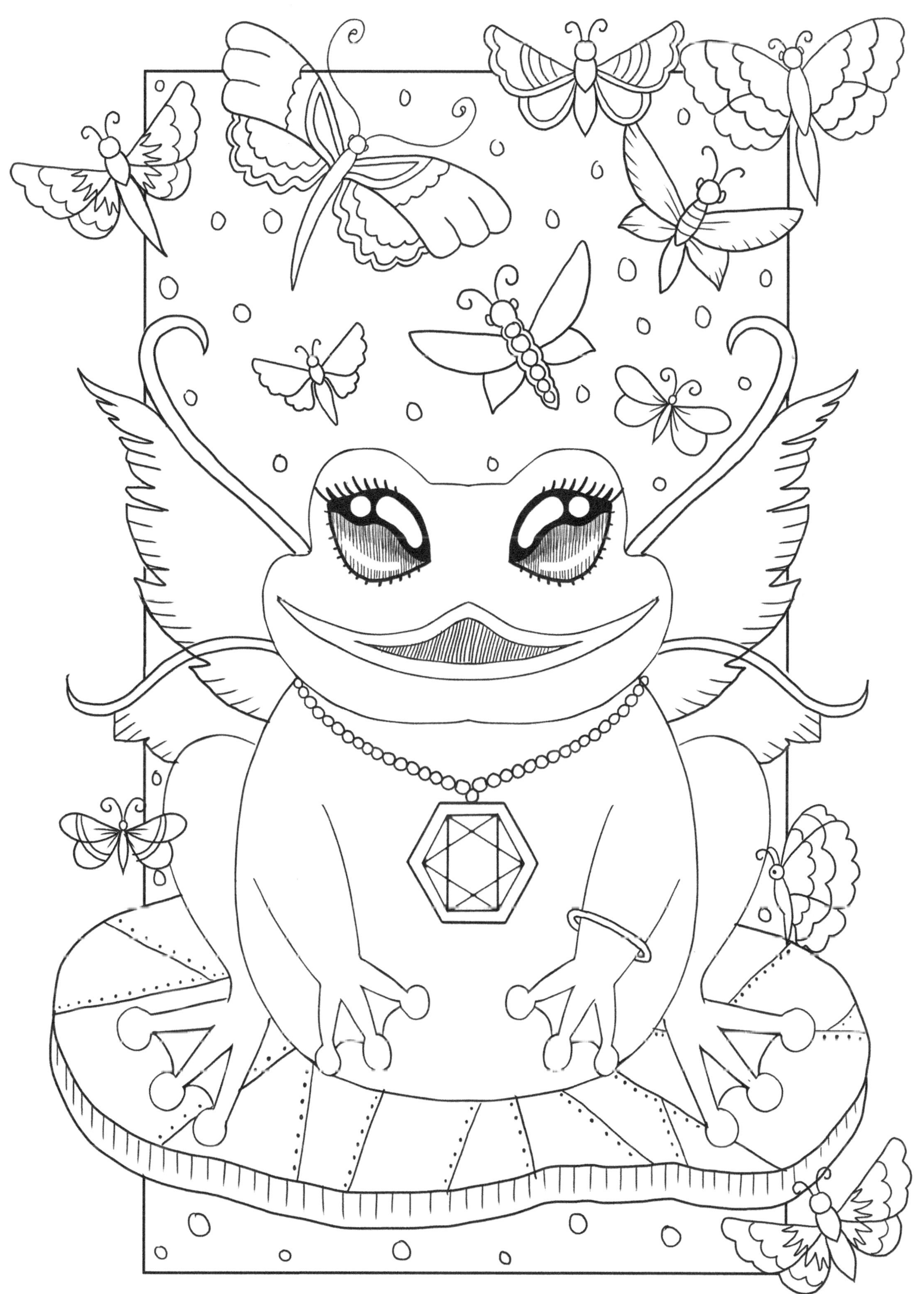

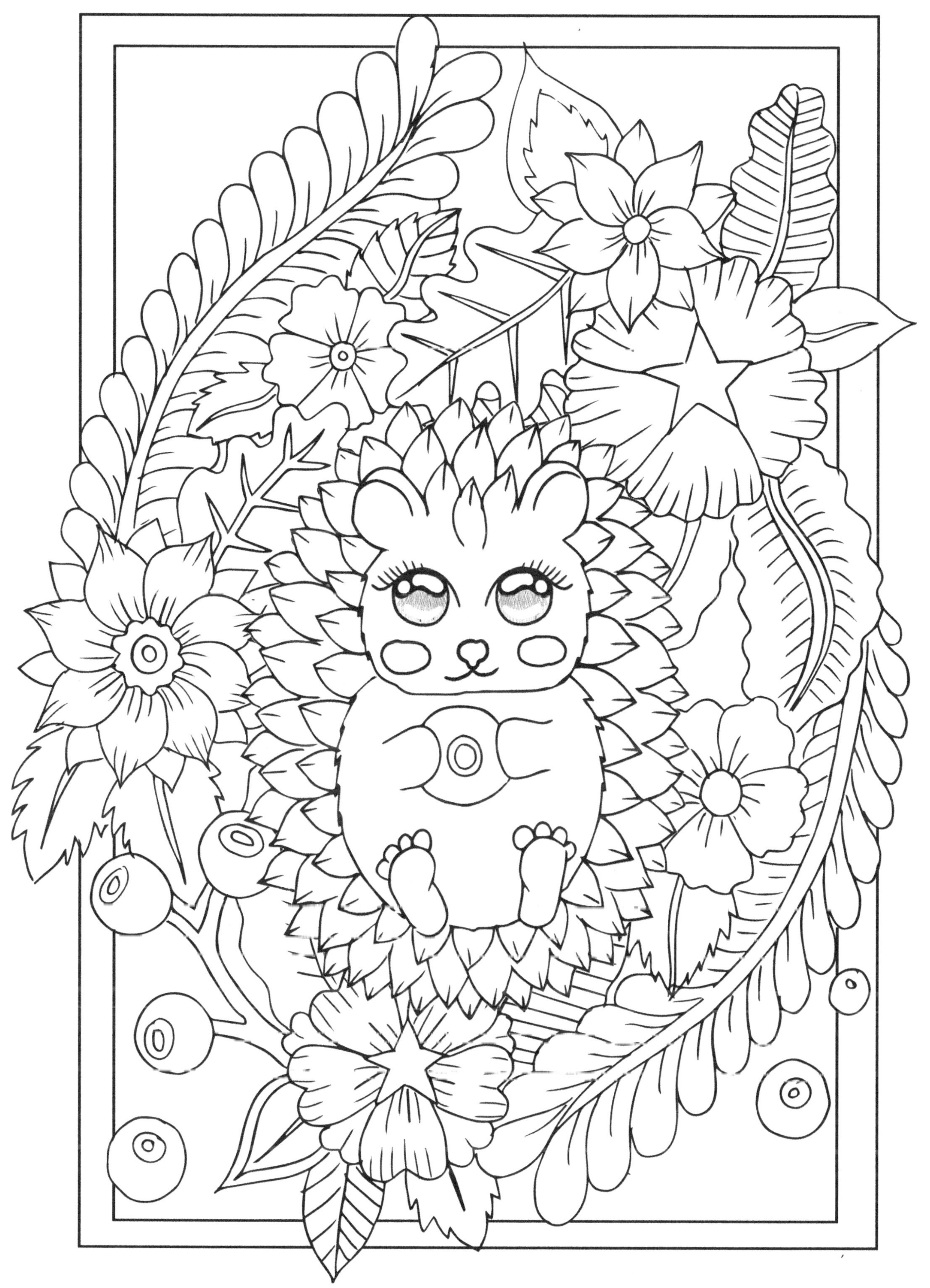

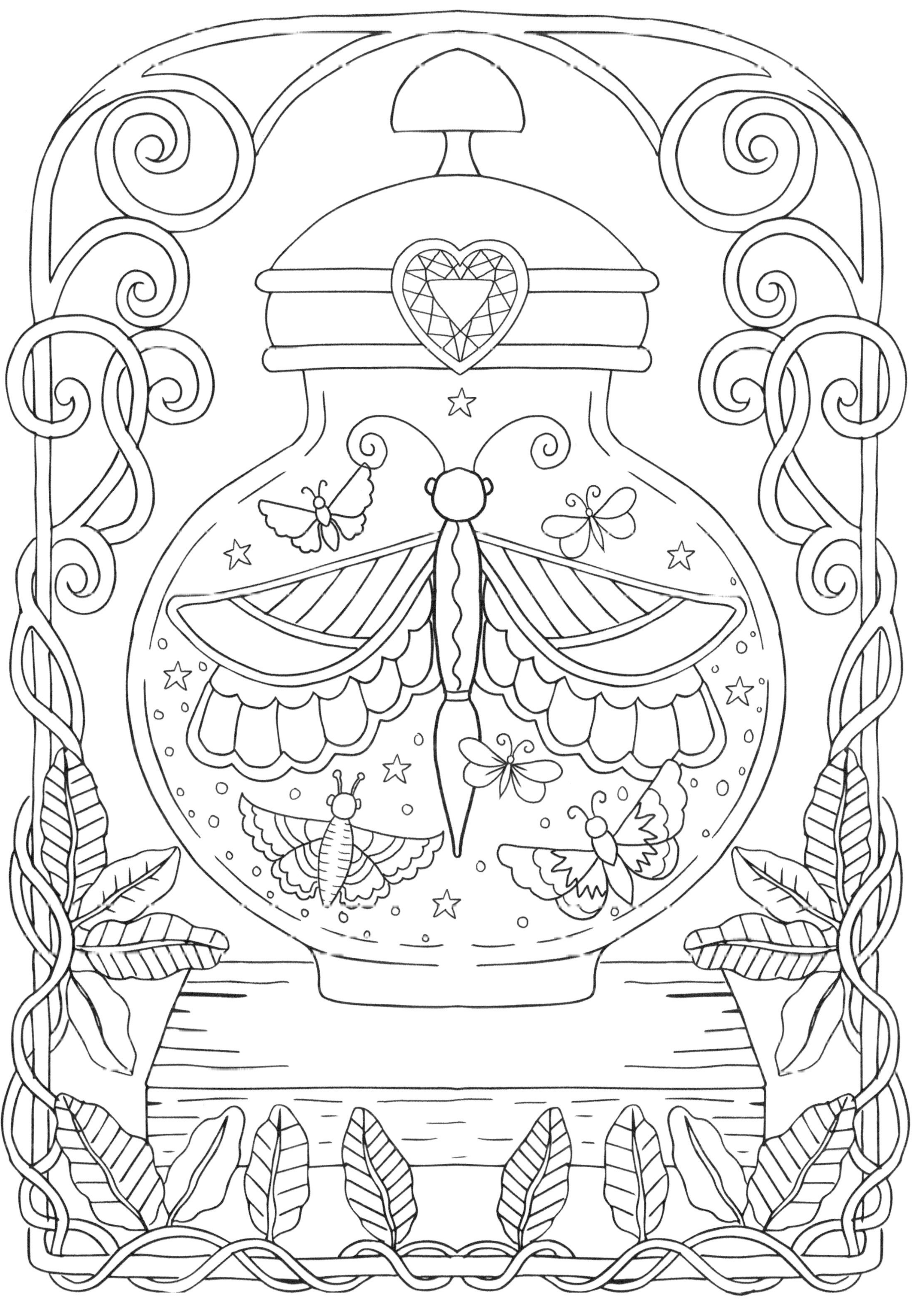

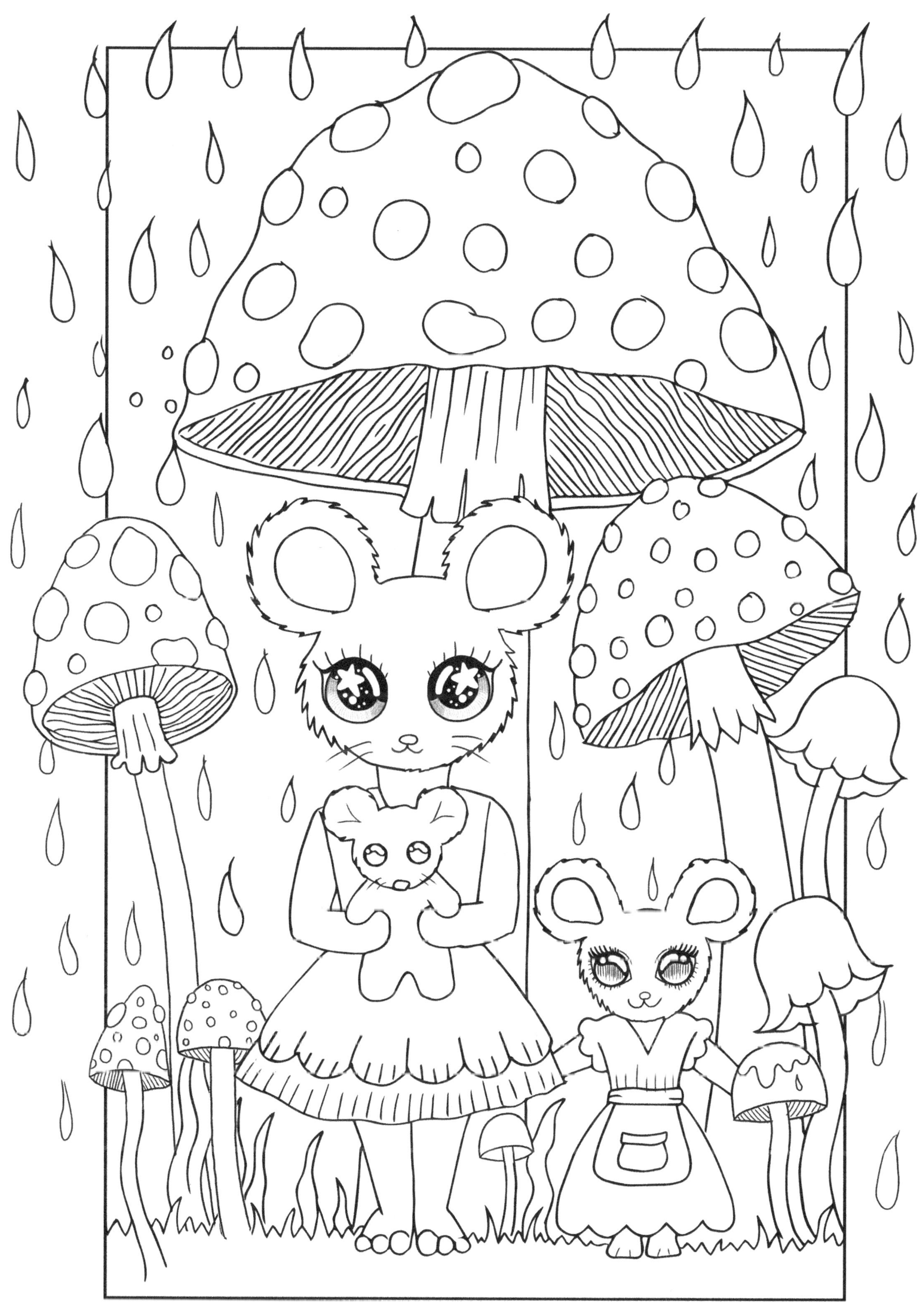

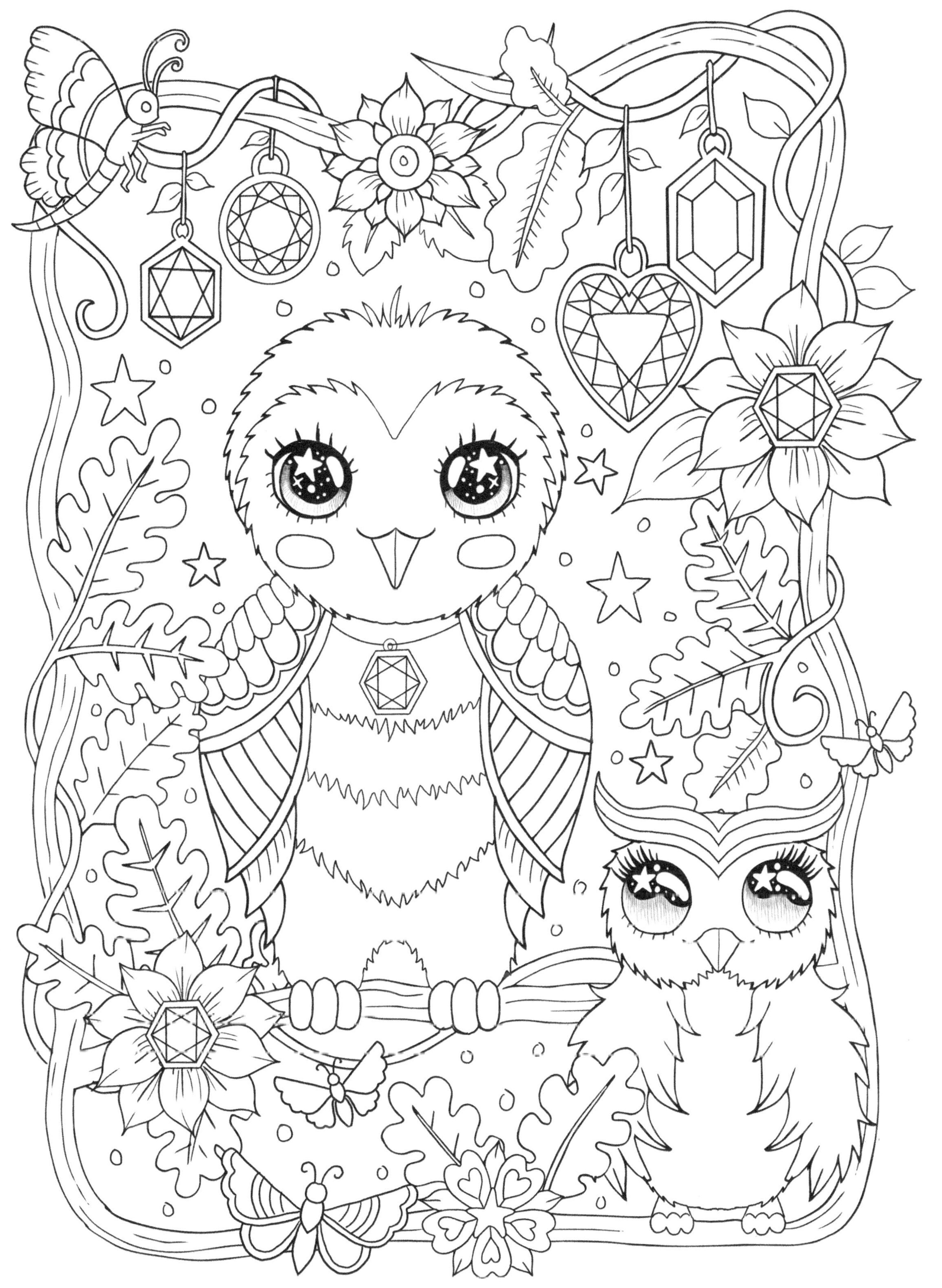

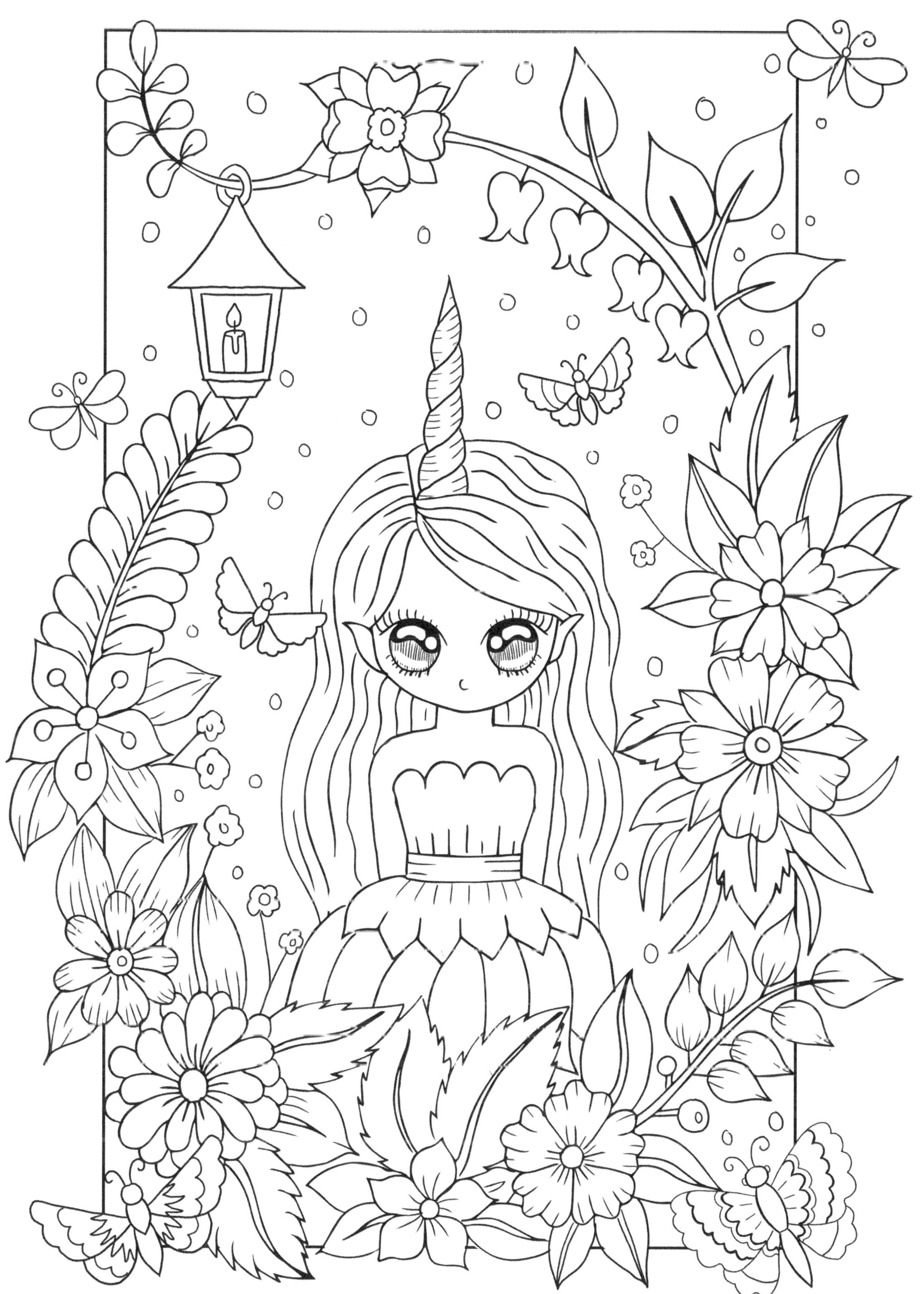

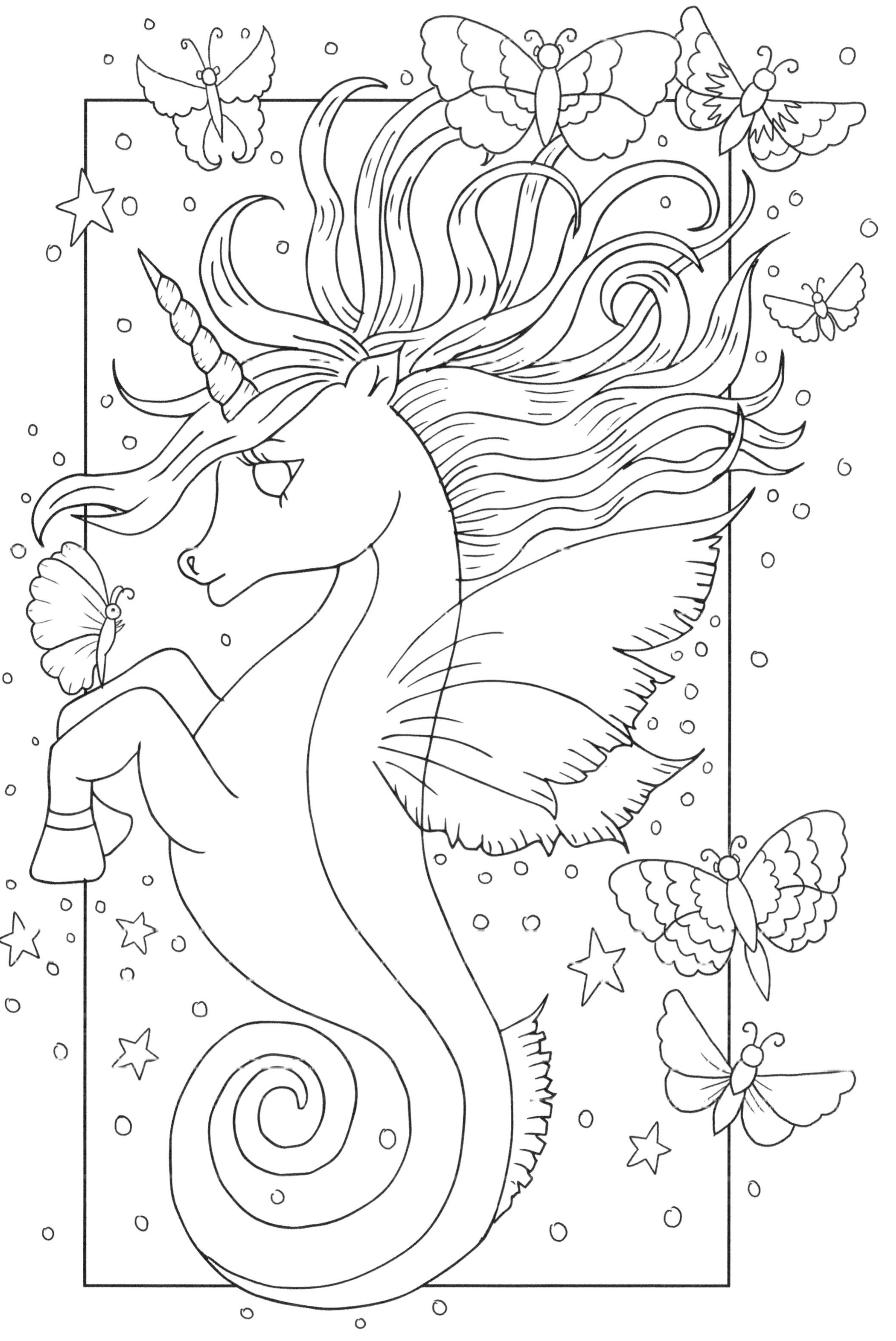

Thank you for purchasing a digital edition of **Dreamlings 3**

by Edwina Mc Namee

You can download the book using the link below:

https://www.edwinamcnamee.com/dreamlings3/

We made the book available using Google Drive. Google Drive allows us to provide high-resolution coloring pages in one PDF file.

All of our books are protected under international copyright law and licensed for your personal use only. You may not share or resell this book. You are welcome to share colored-in pages on social media.

Please let us know if you have any questions:

EDWINAMCNAMEE.COM

Thank you,

Edwina Mc Namee

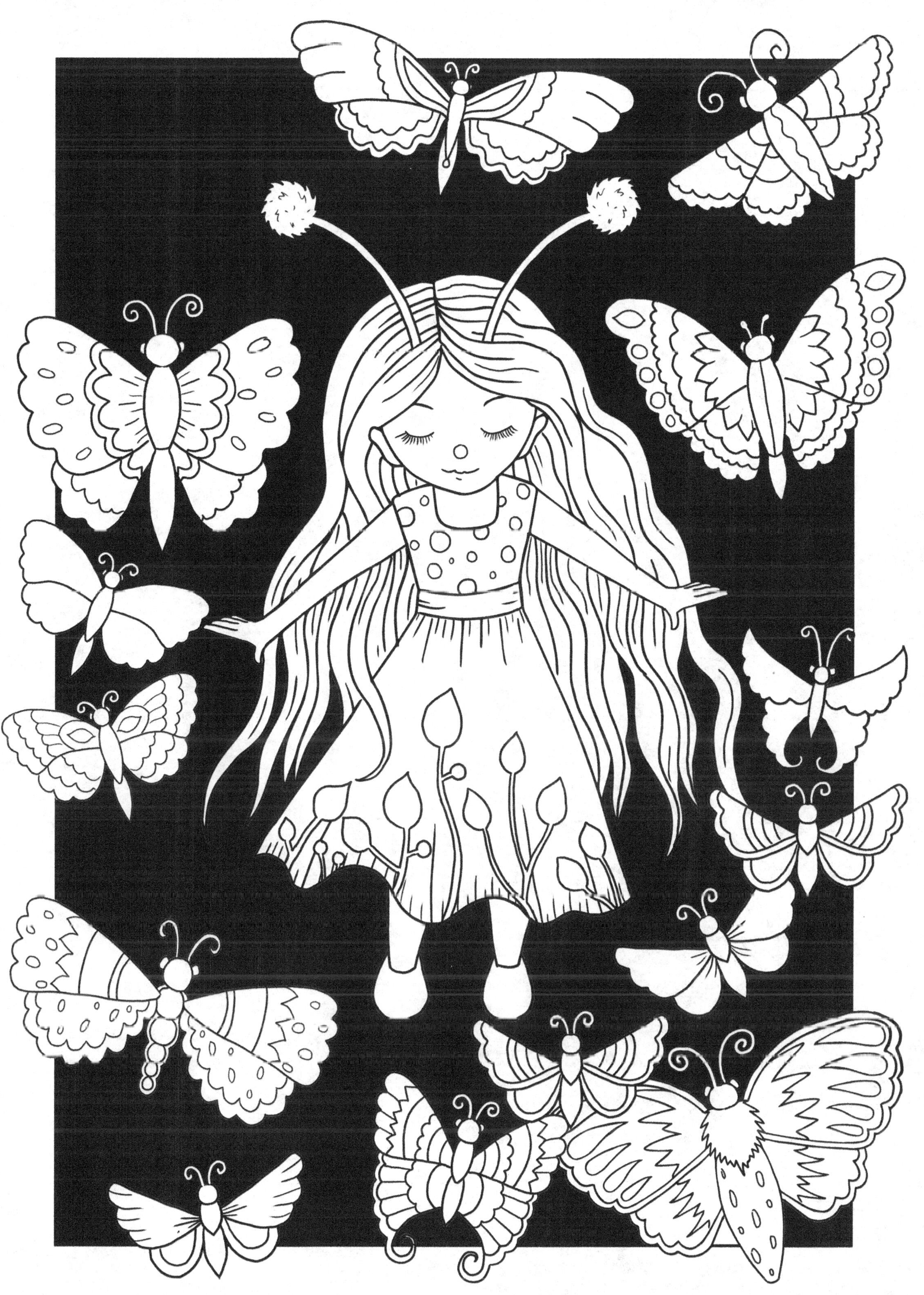

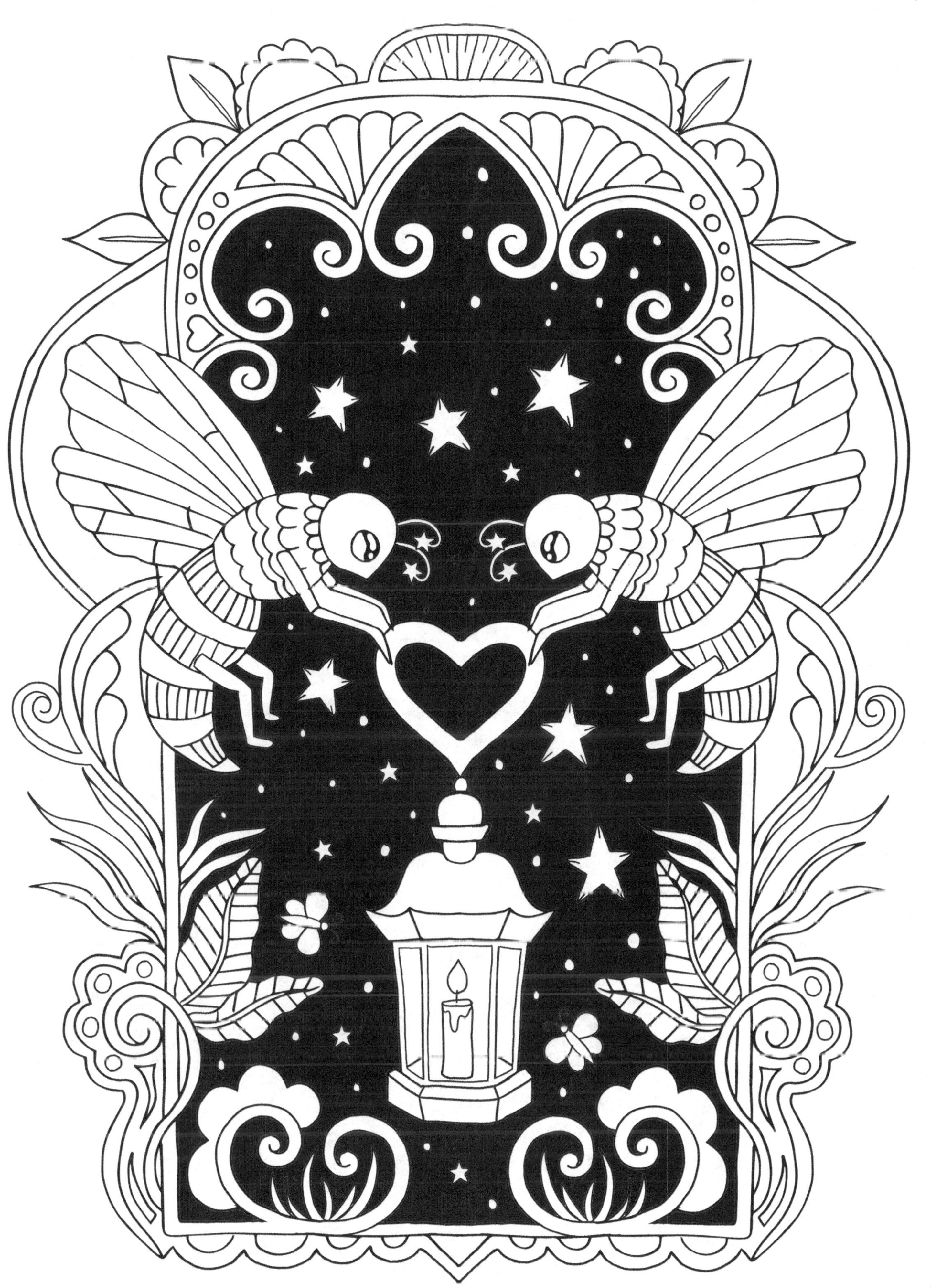

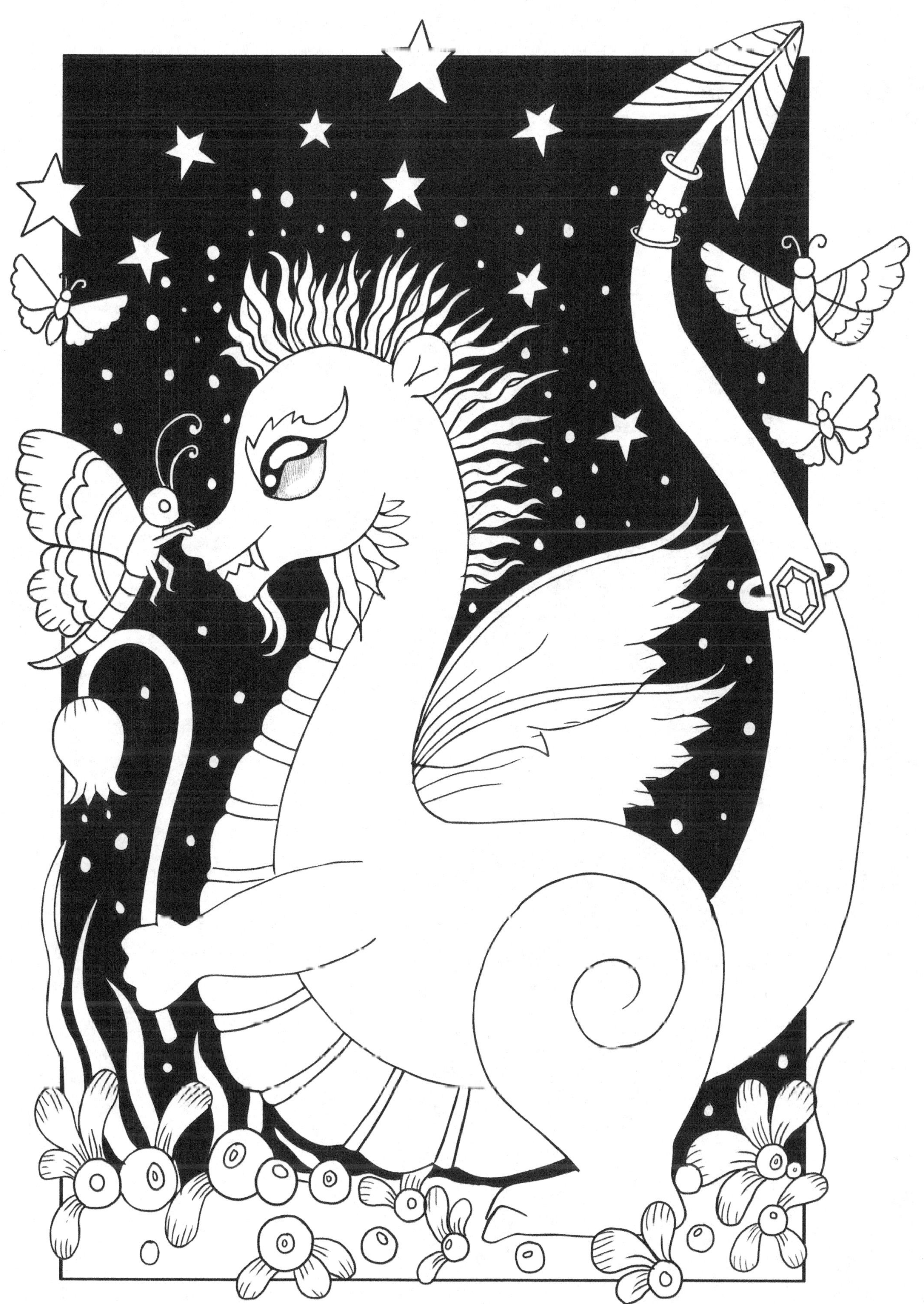

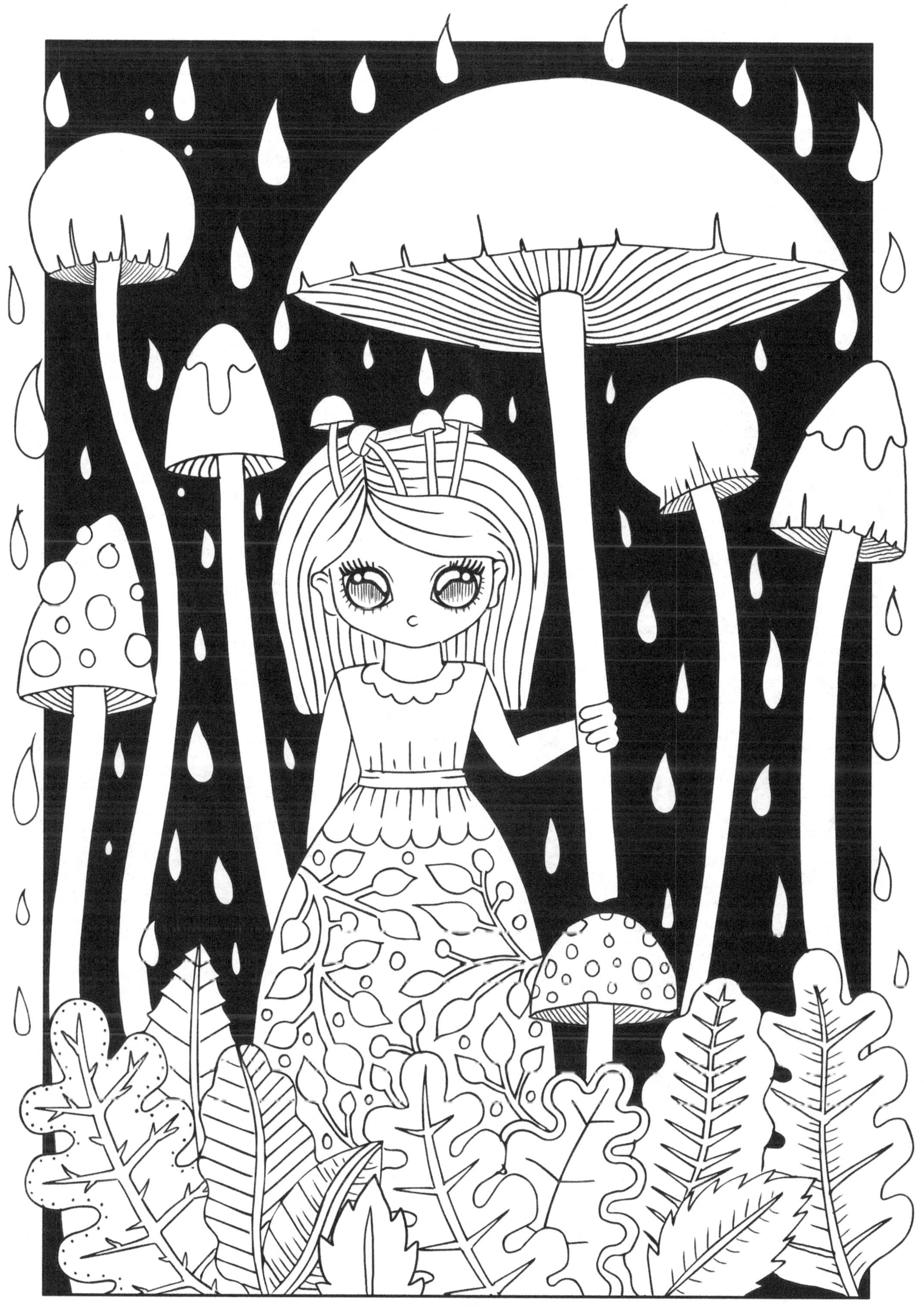

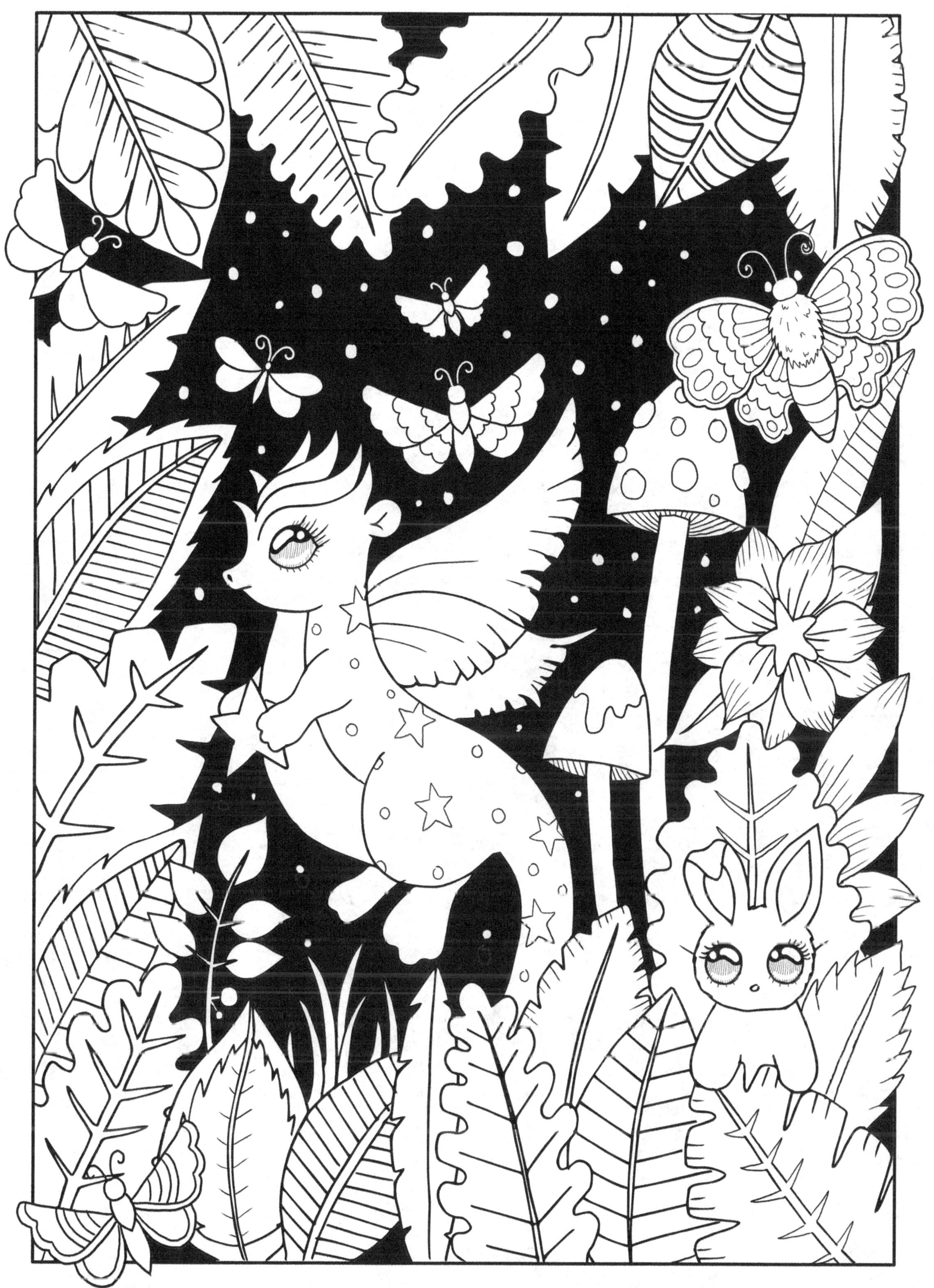

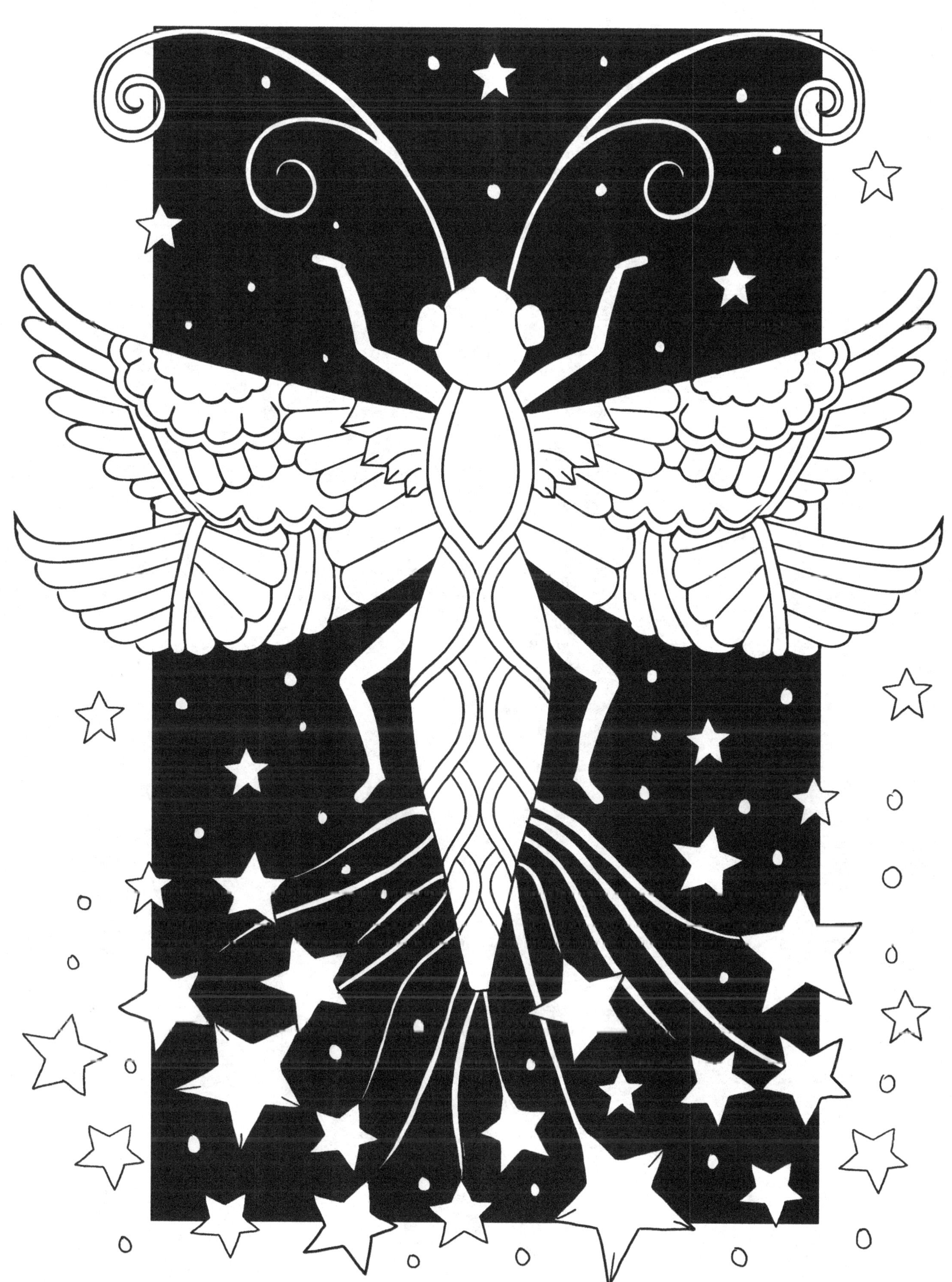

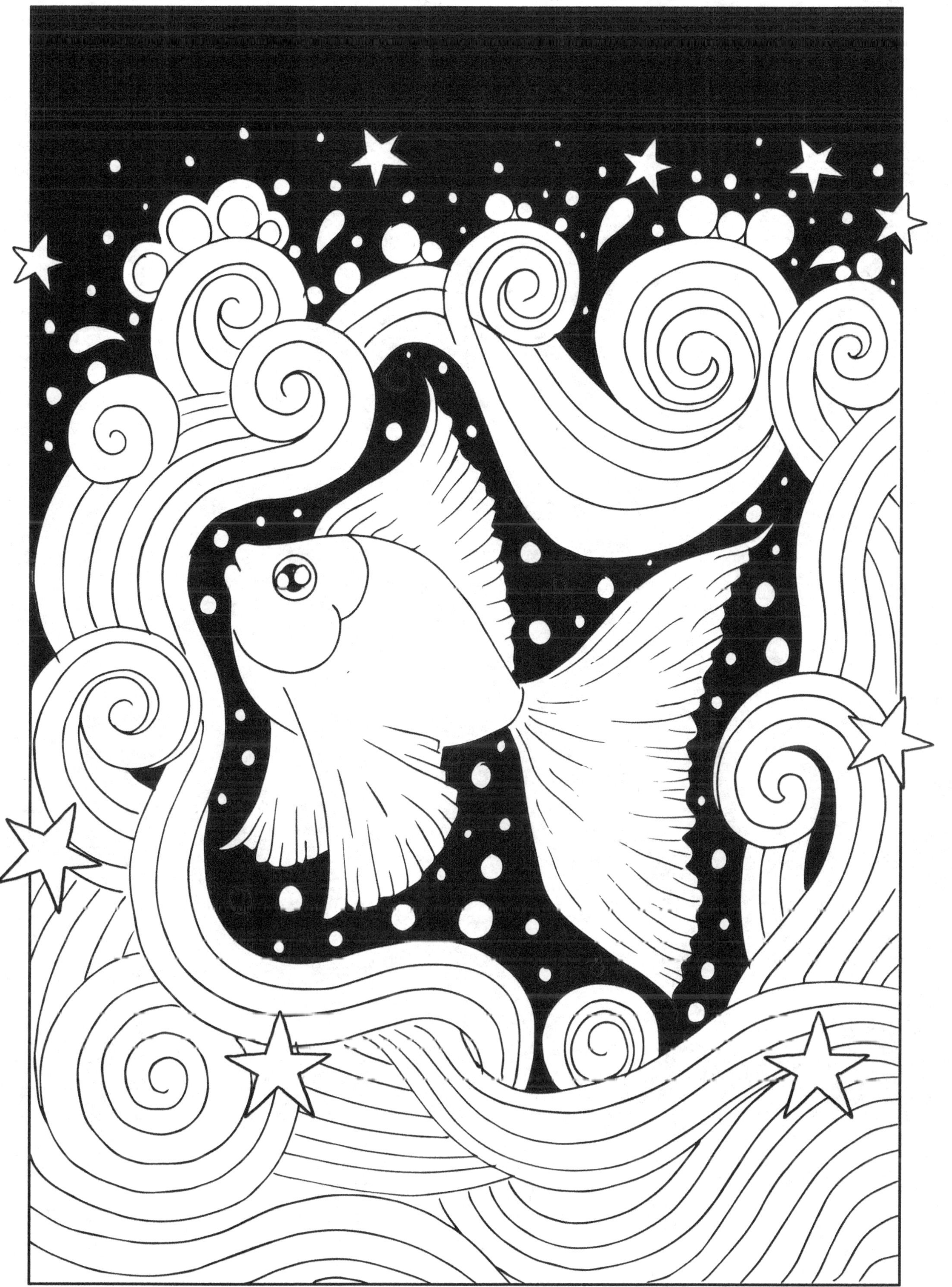

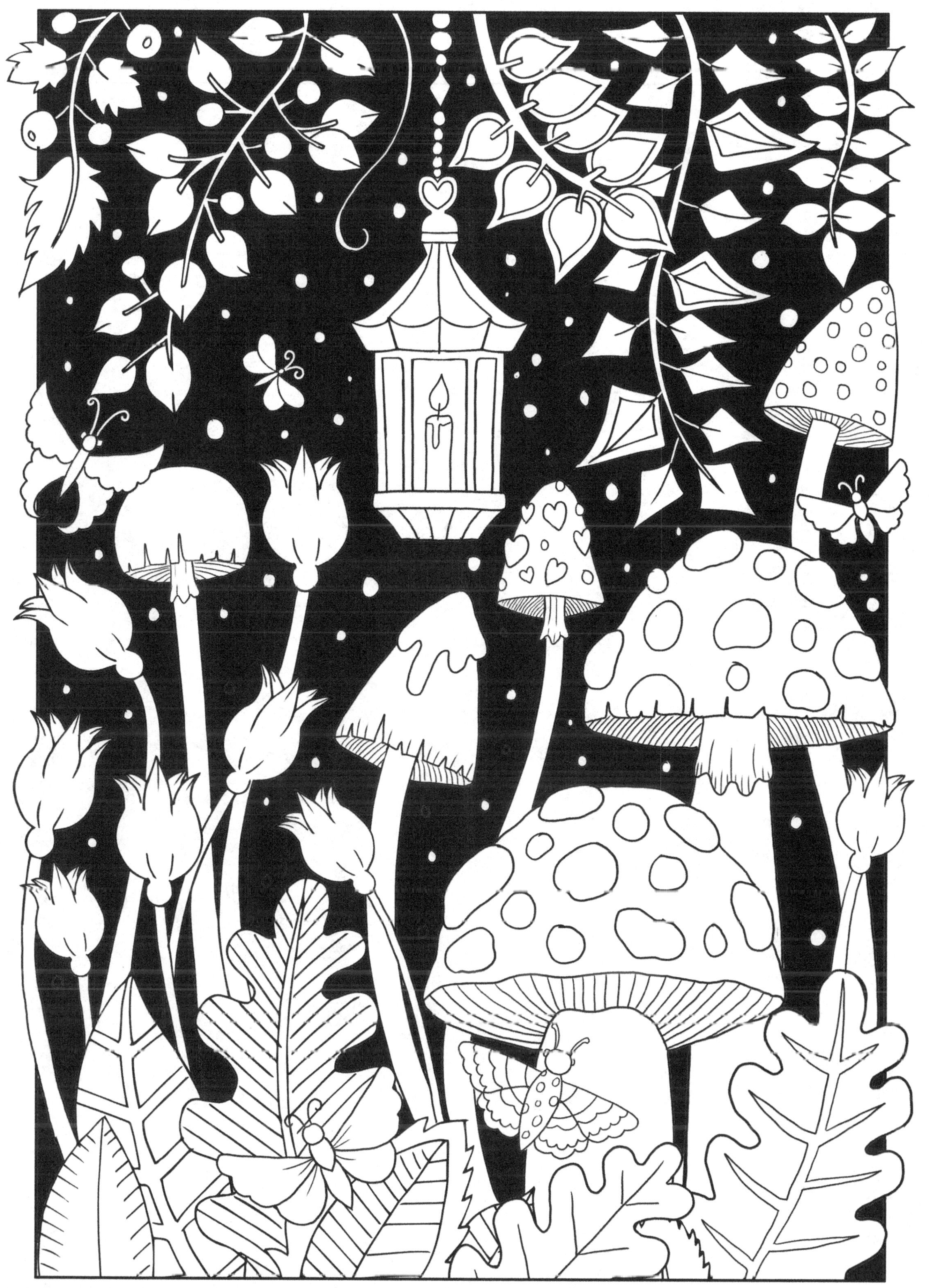

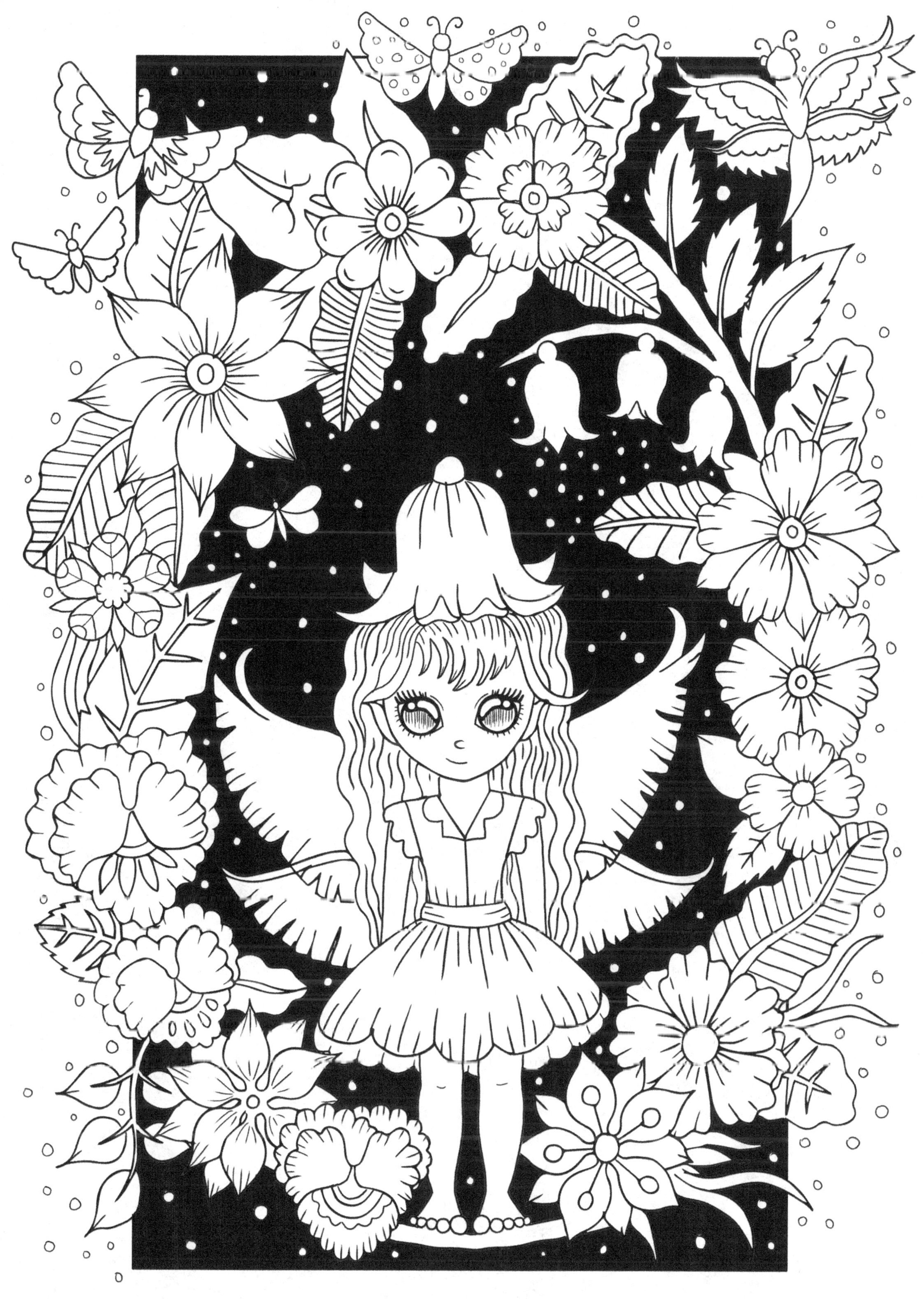

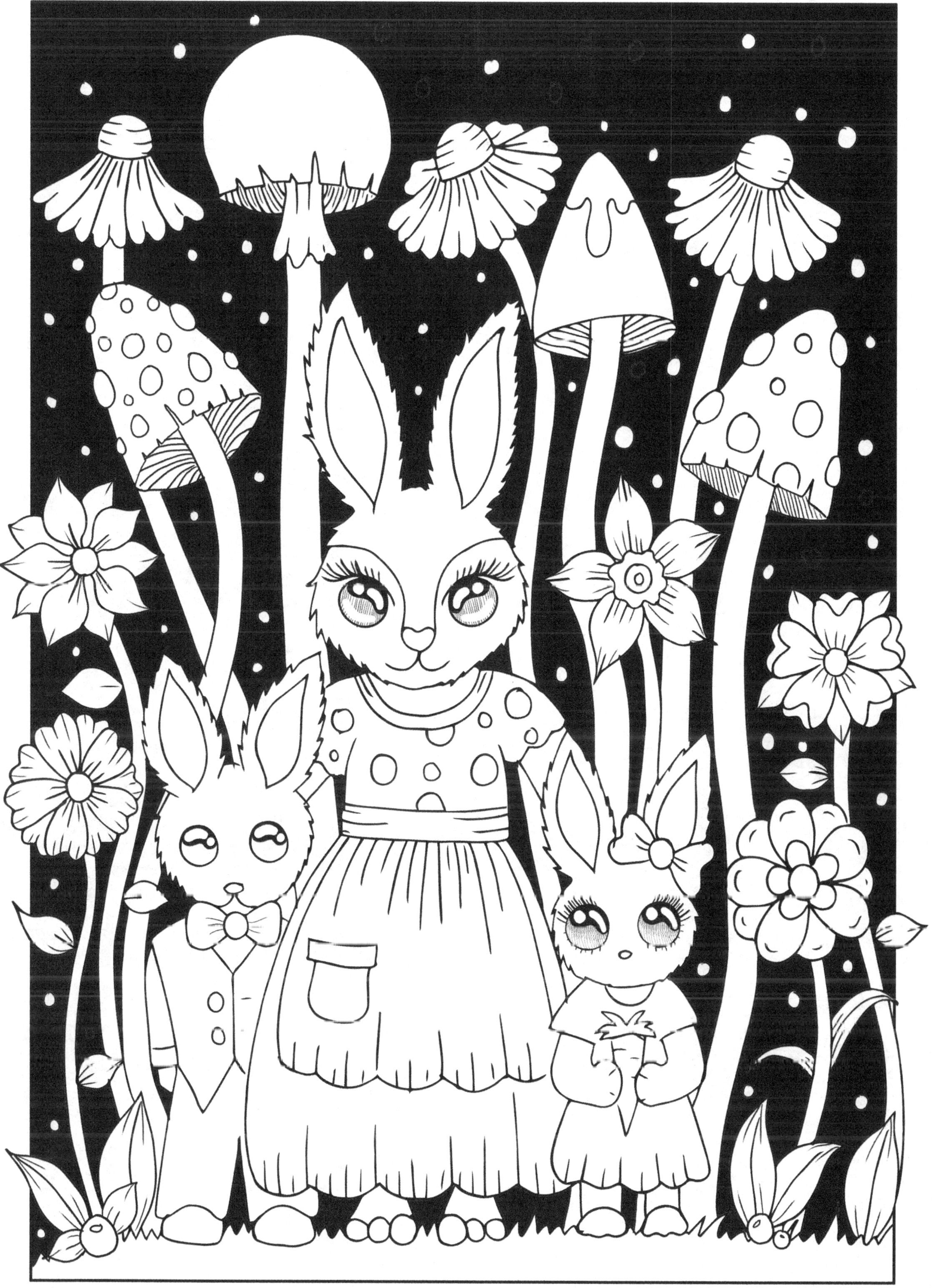

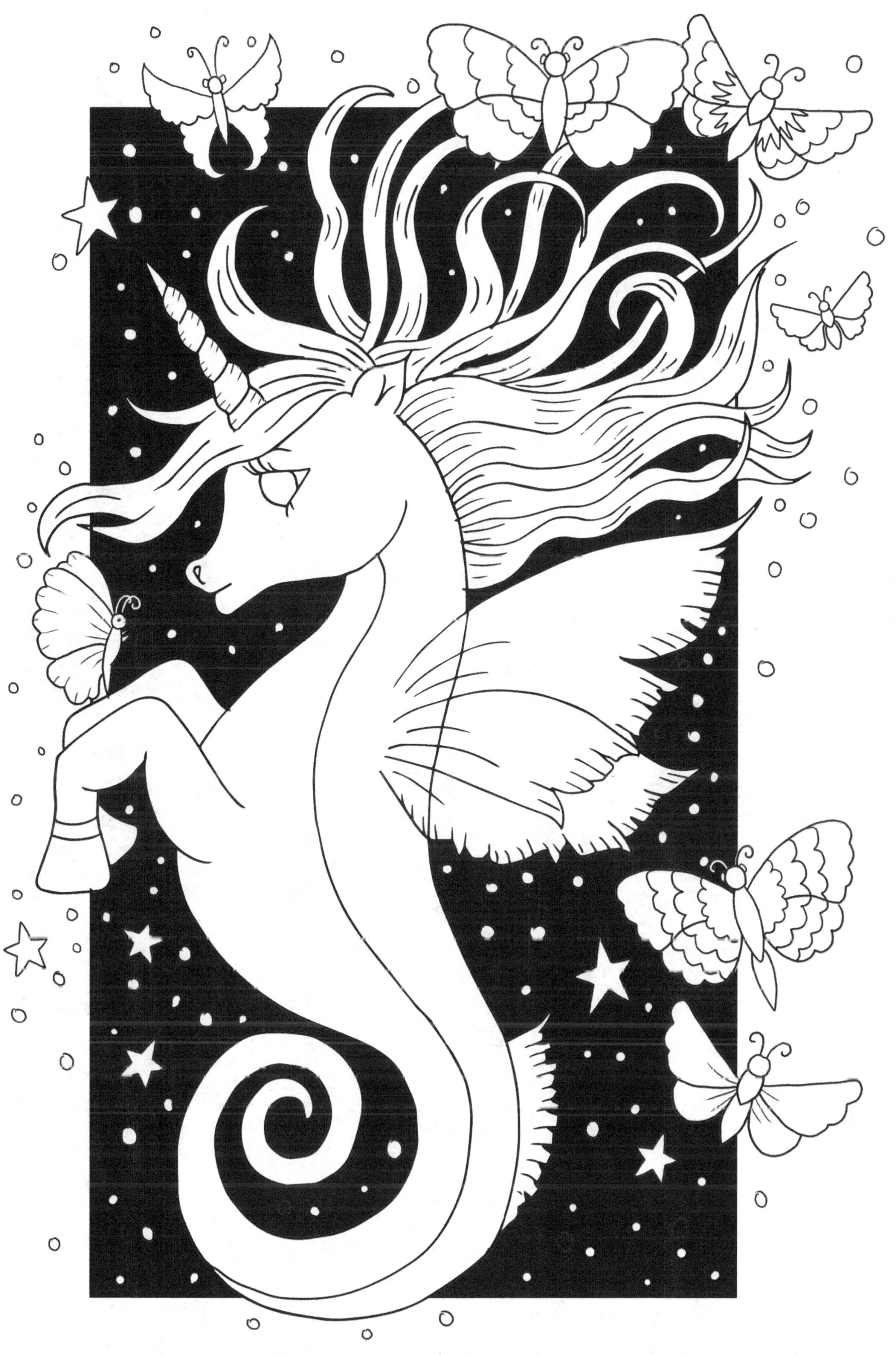

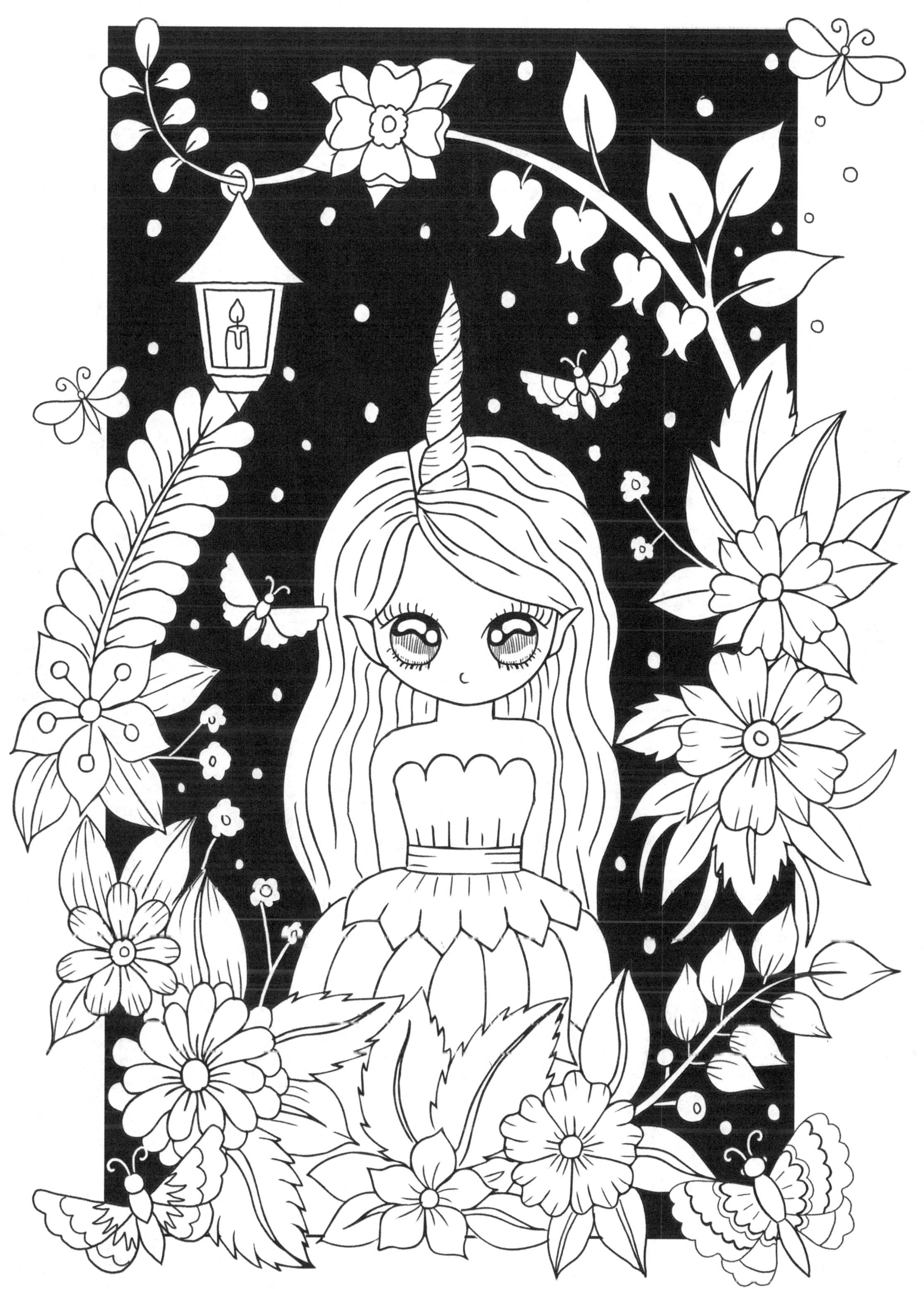

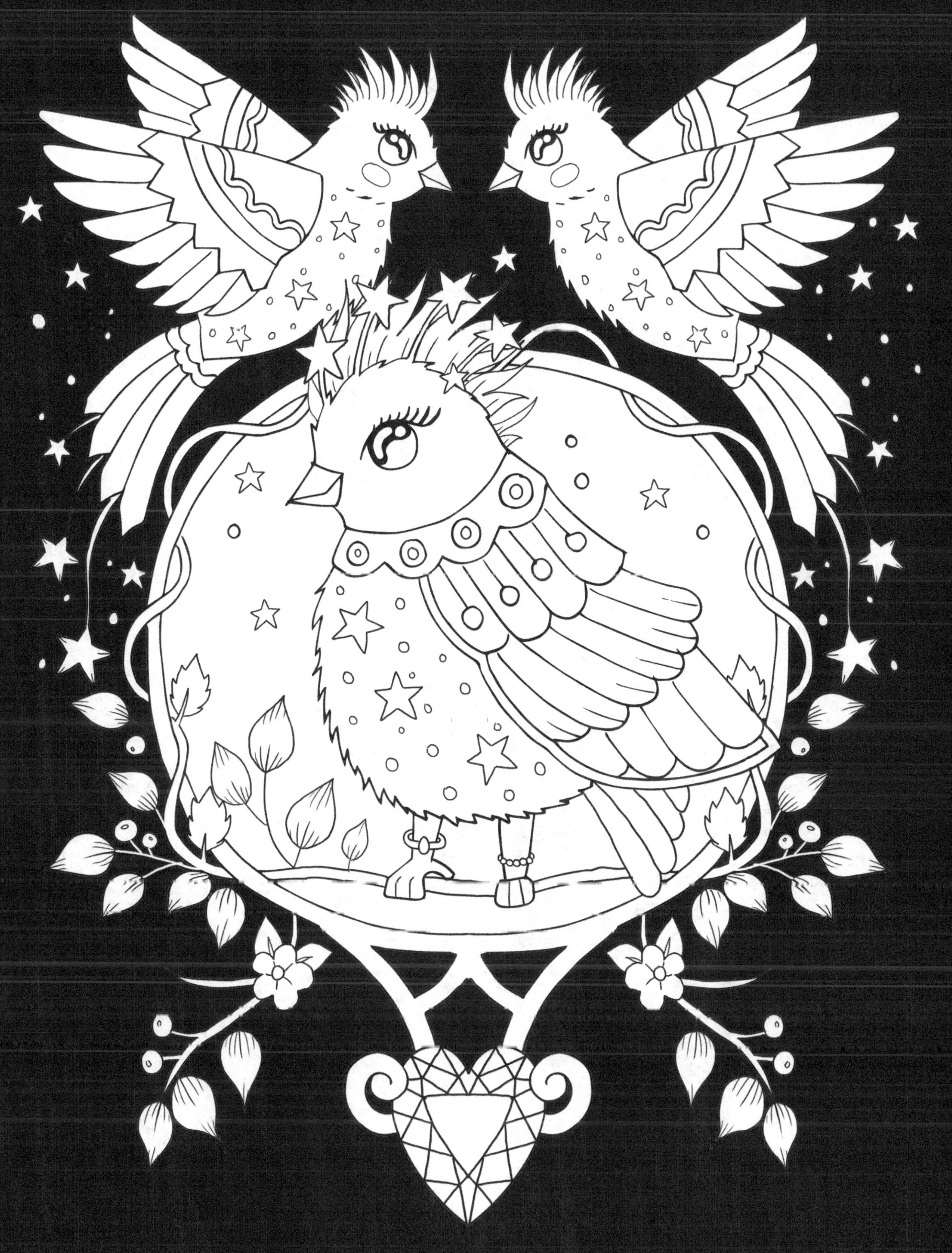

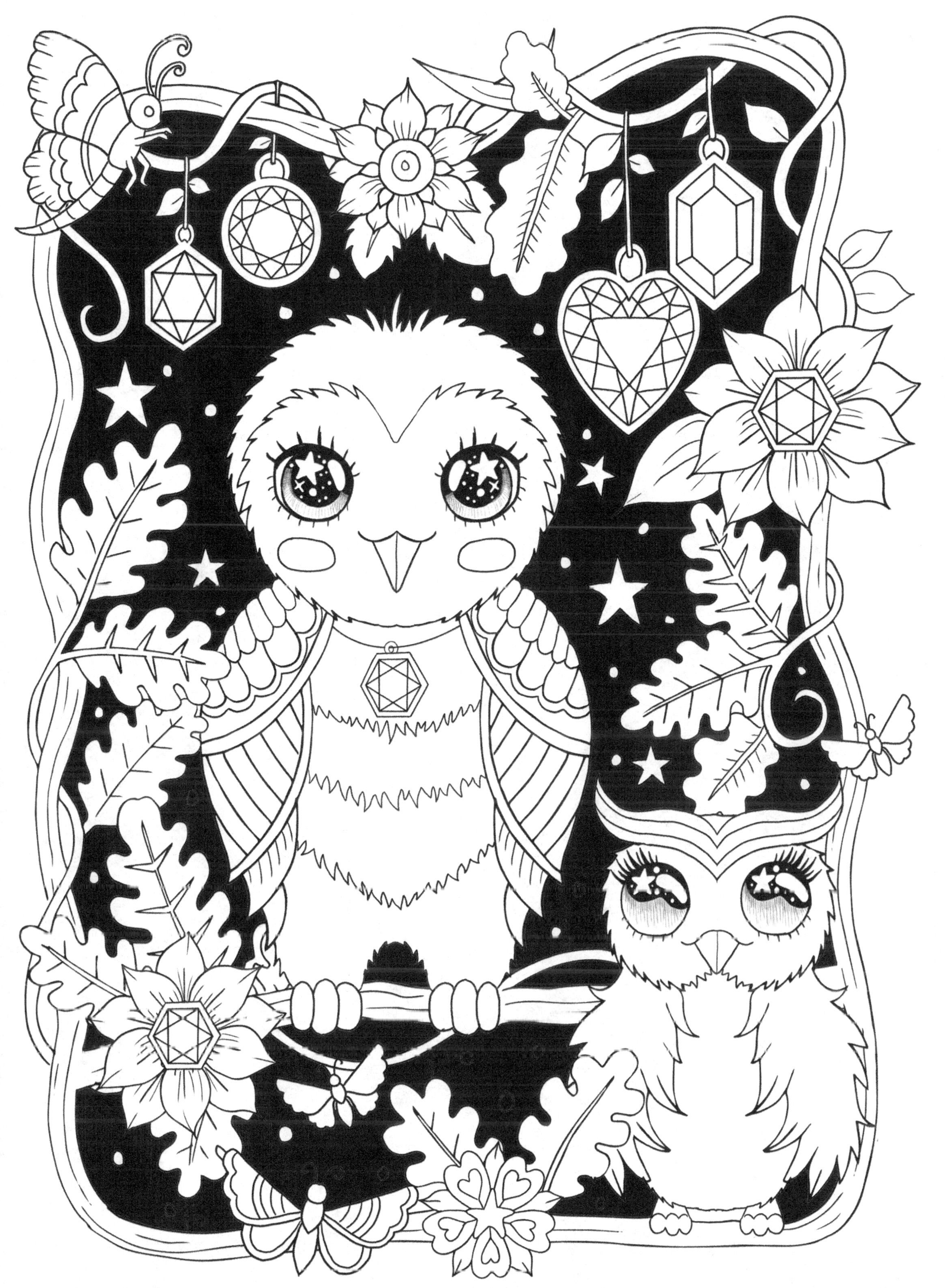

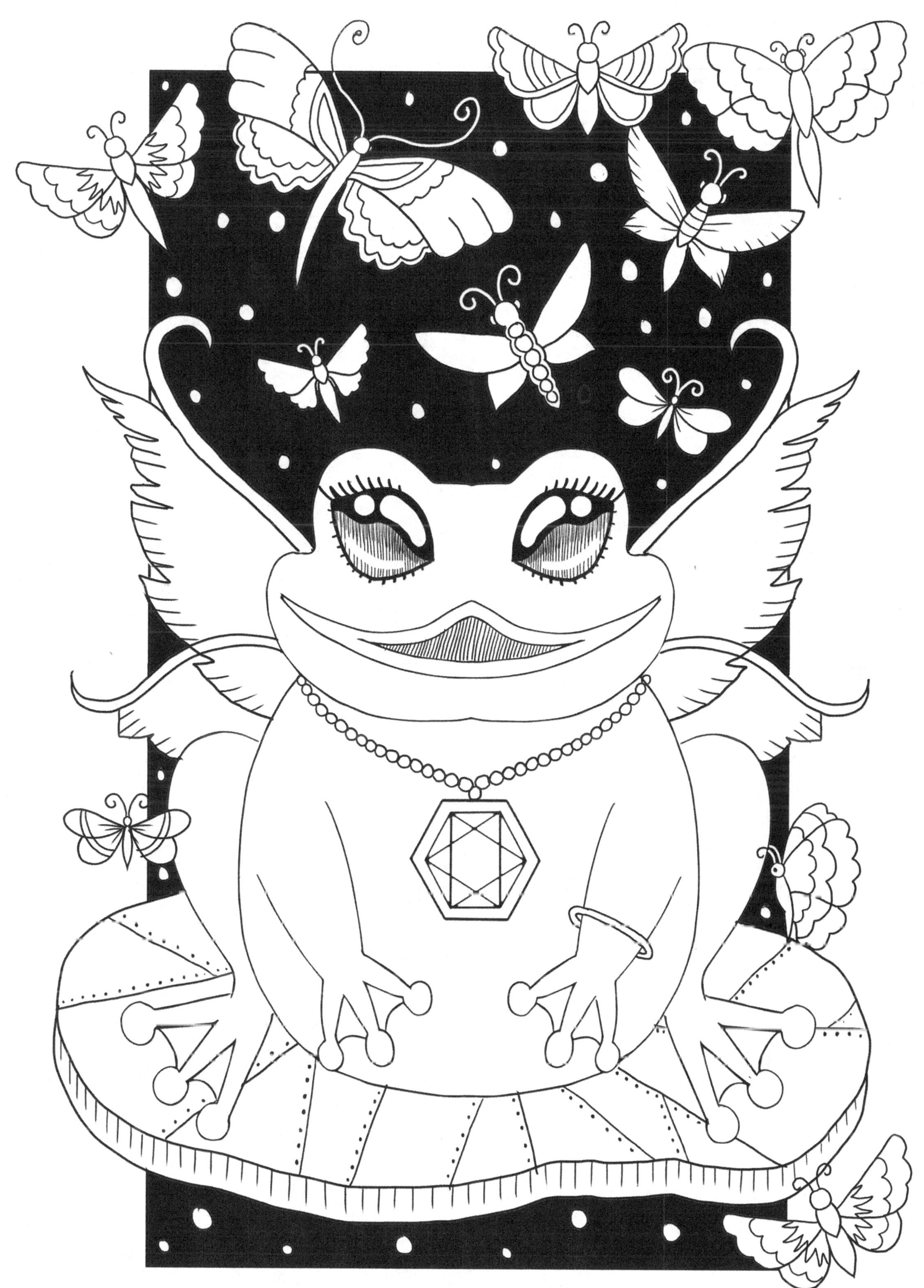

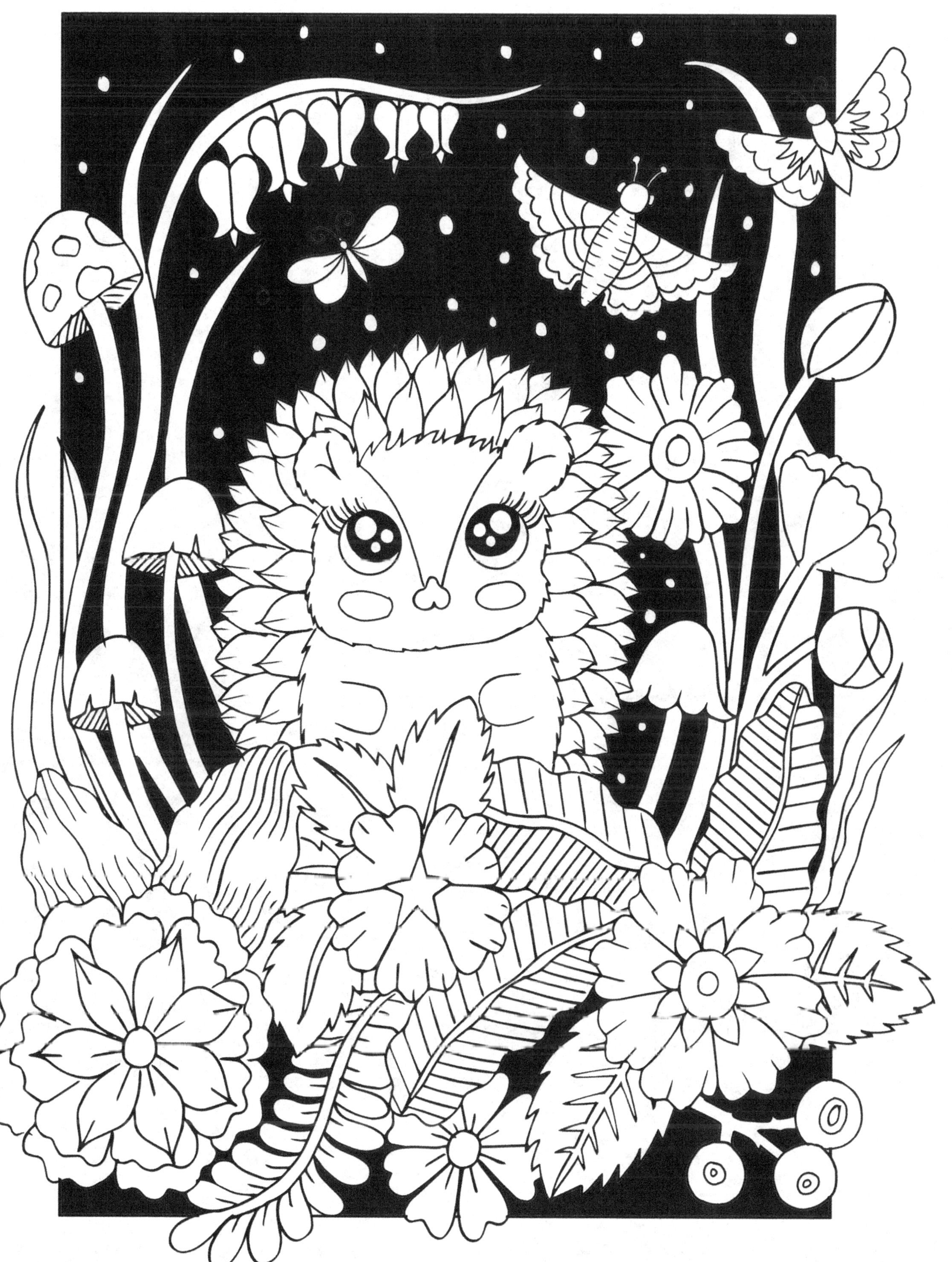

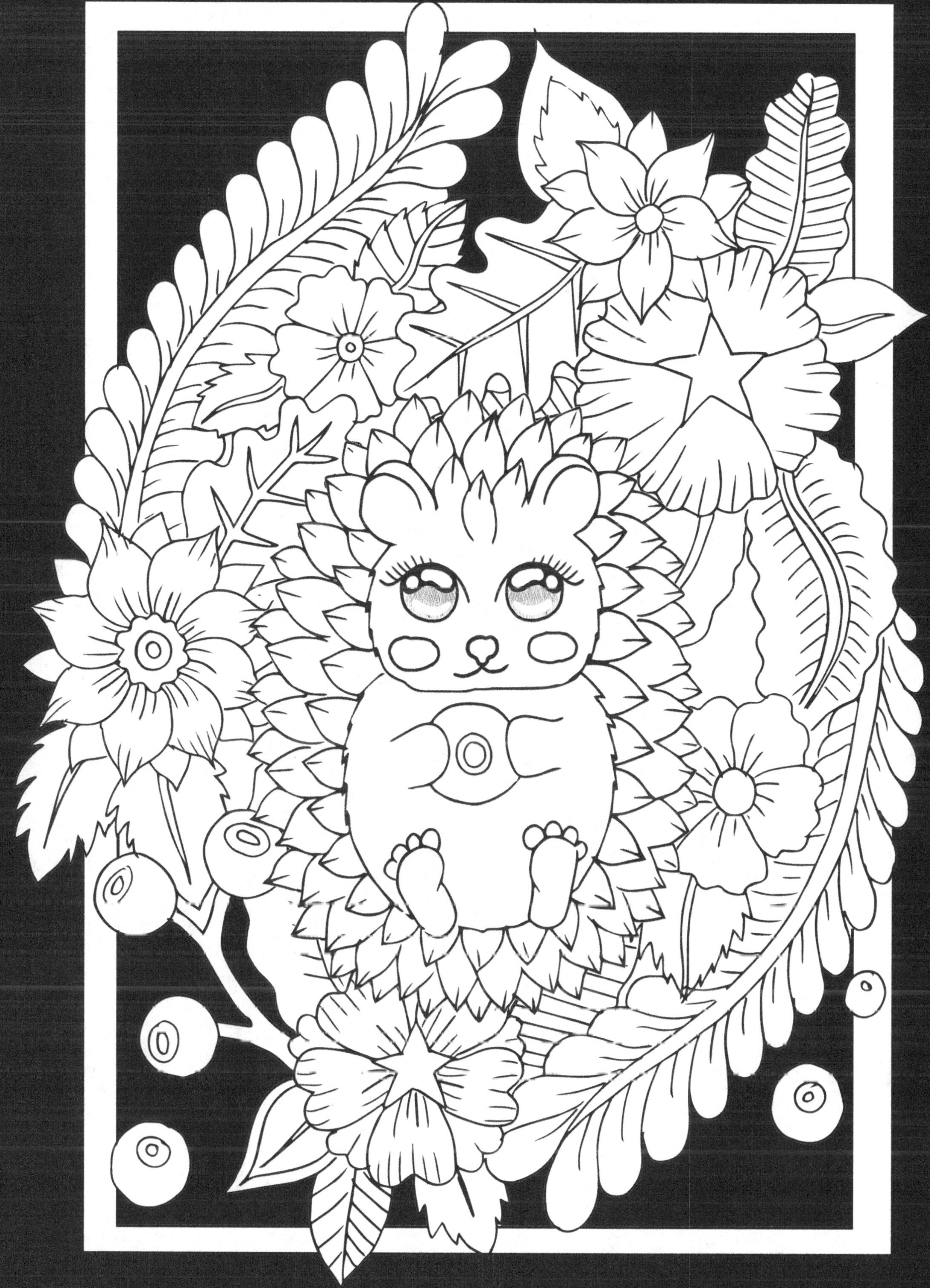

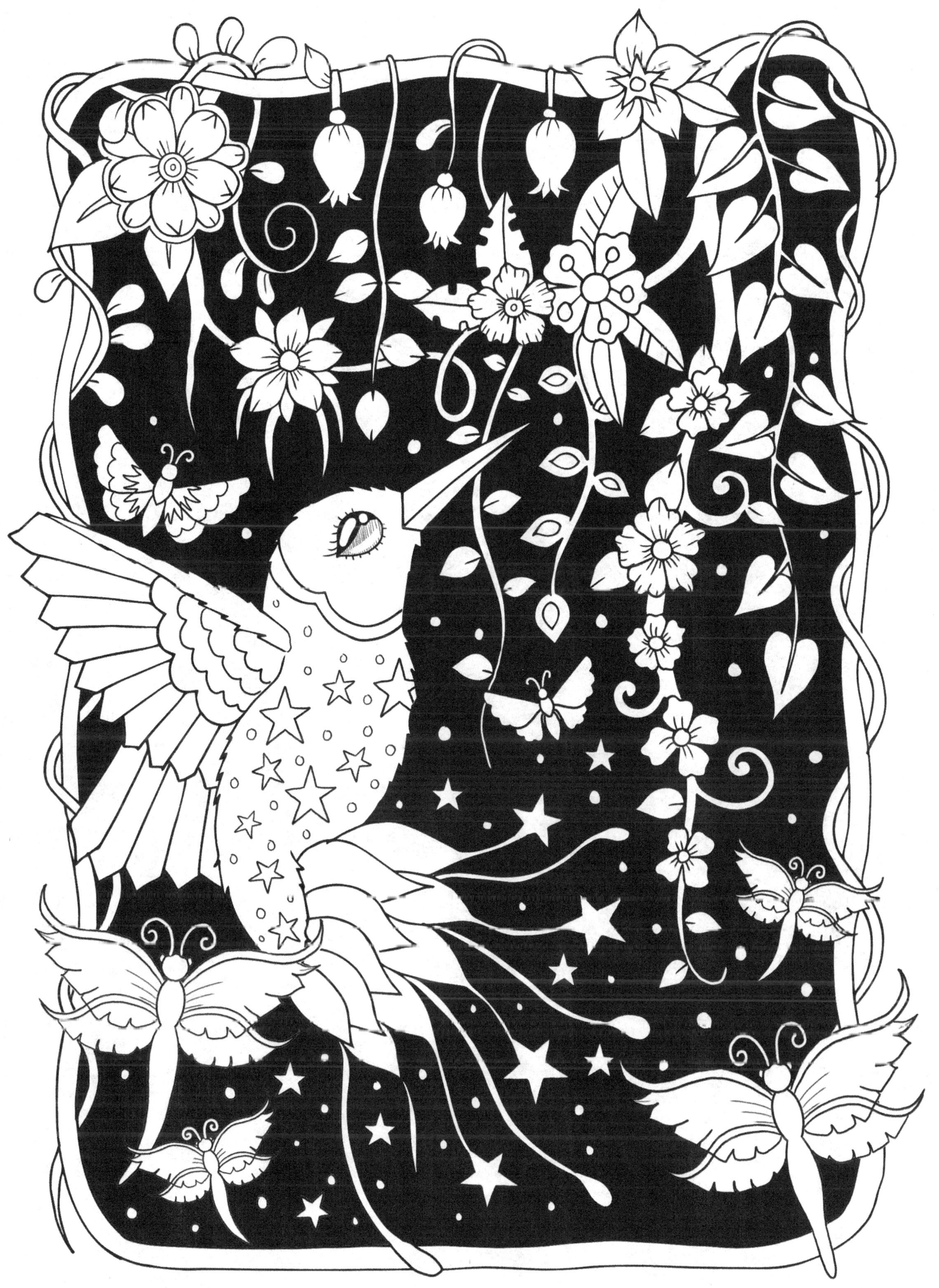

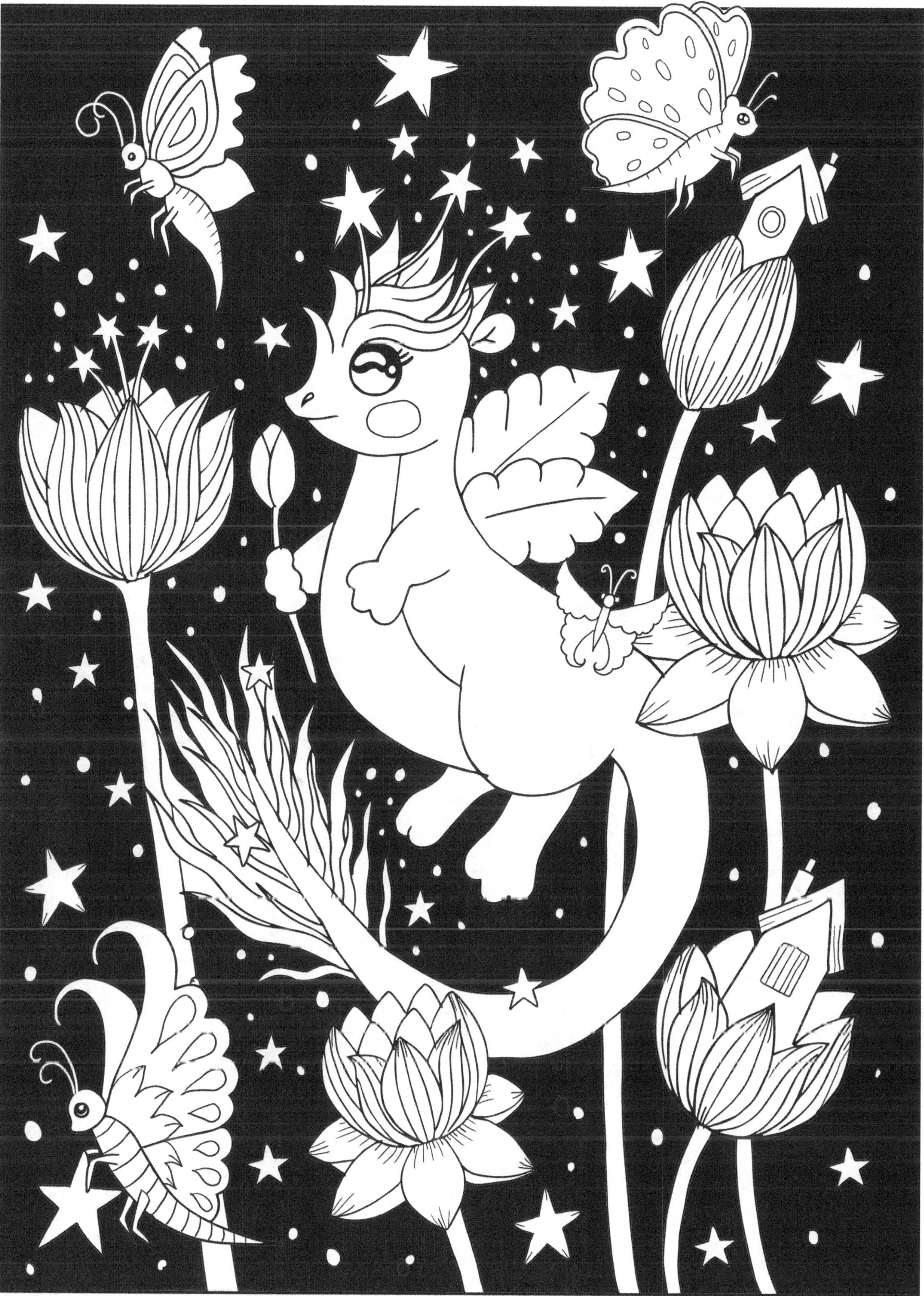

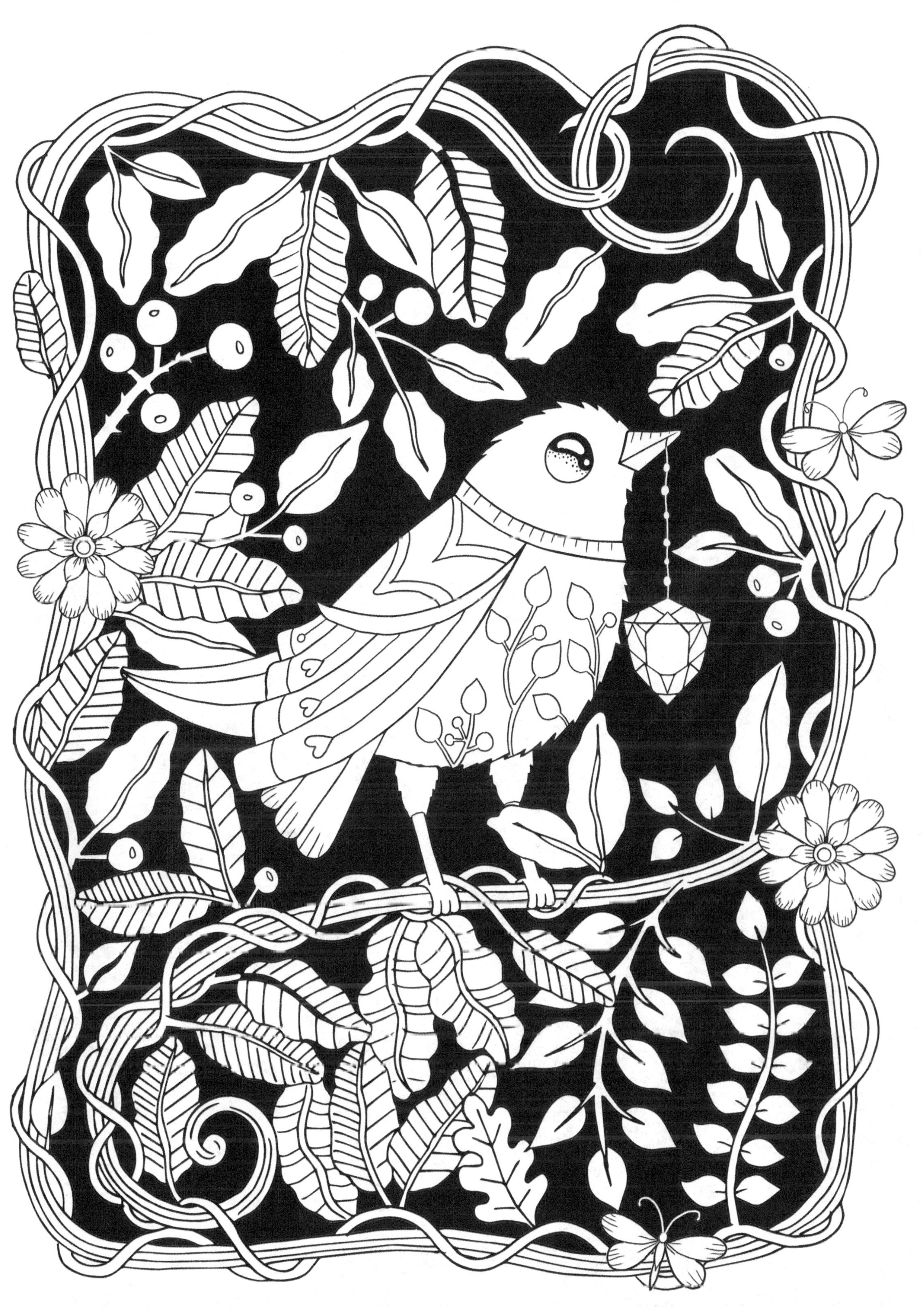

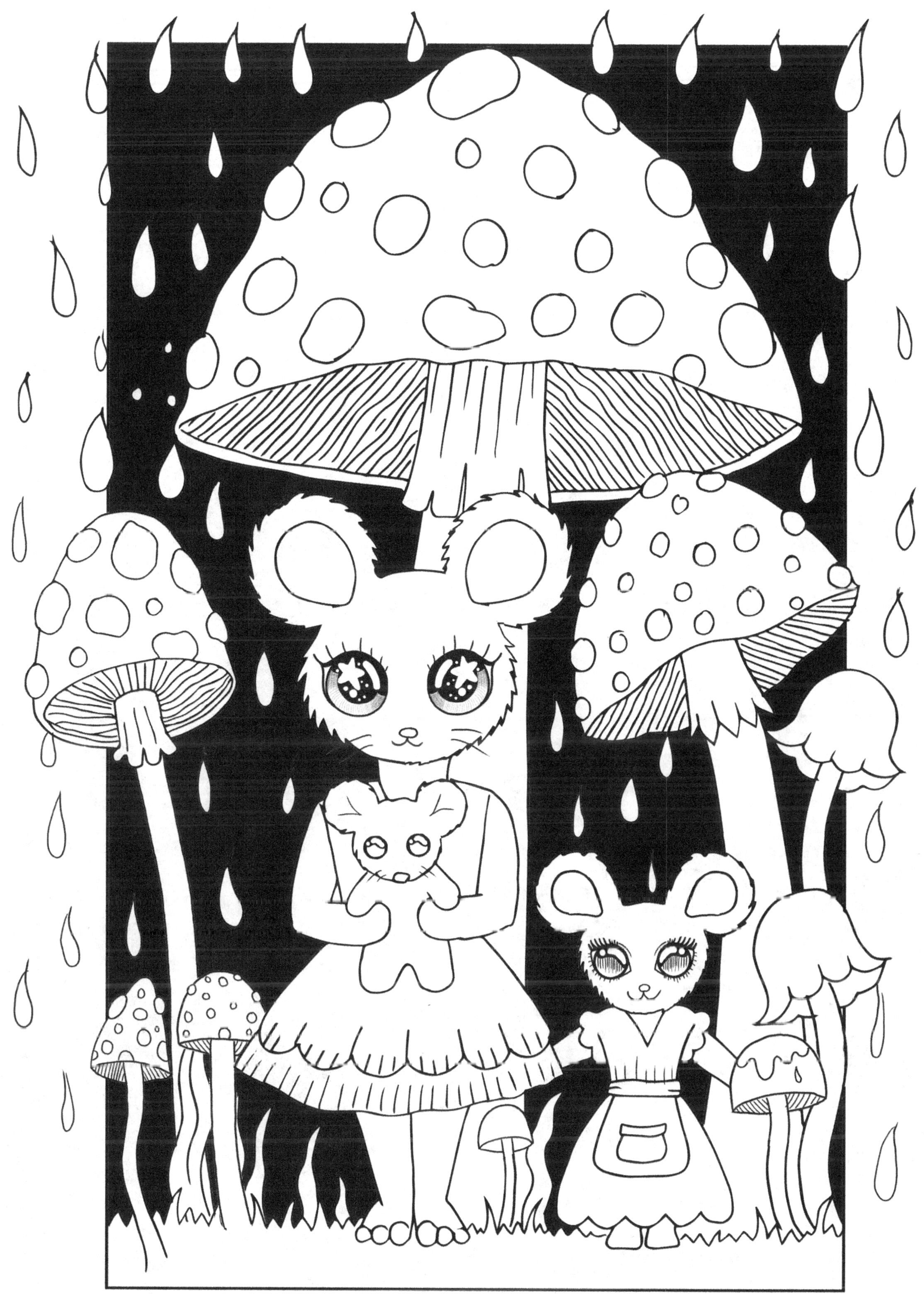

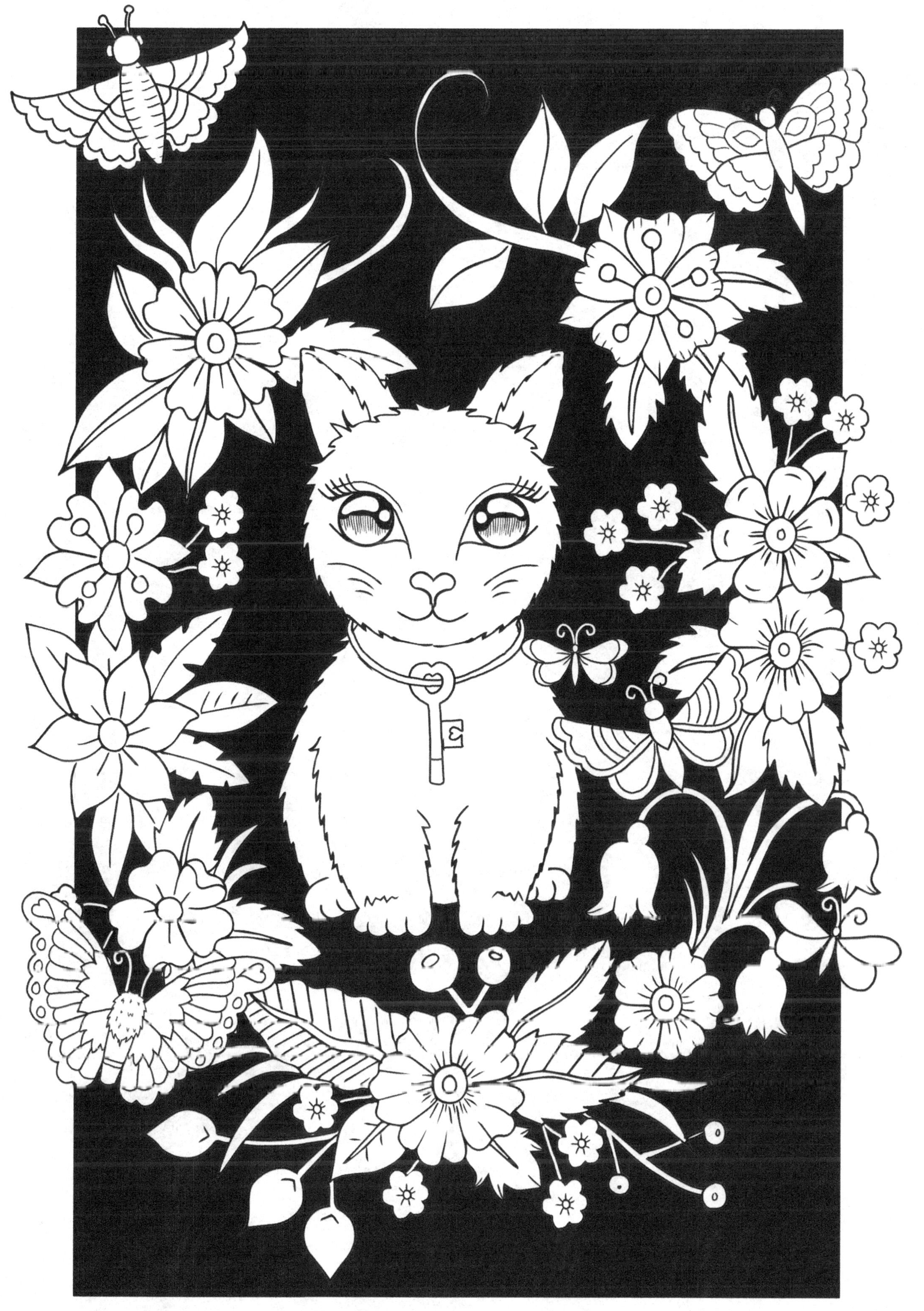

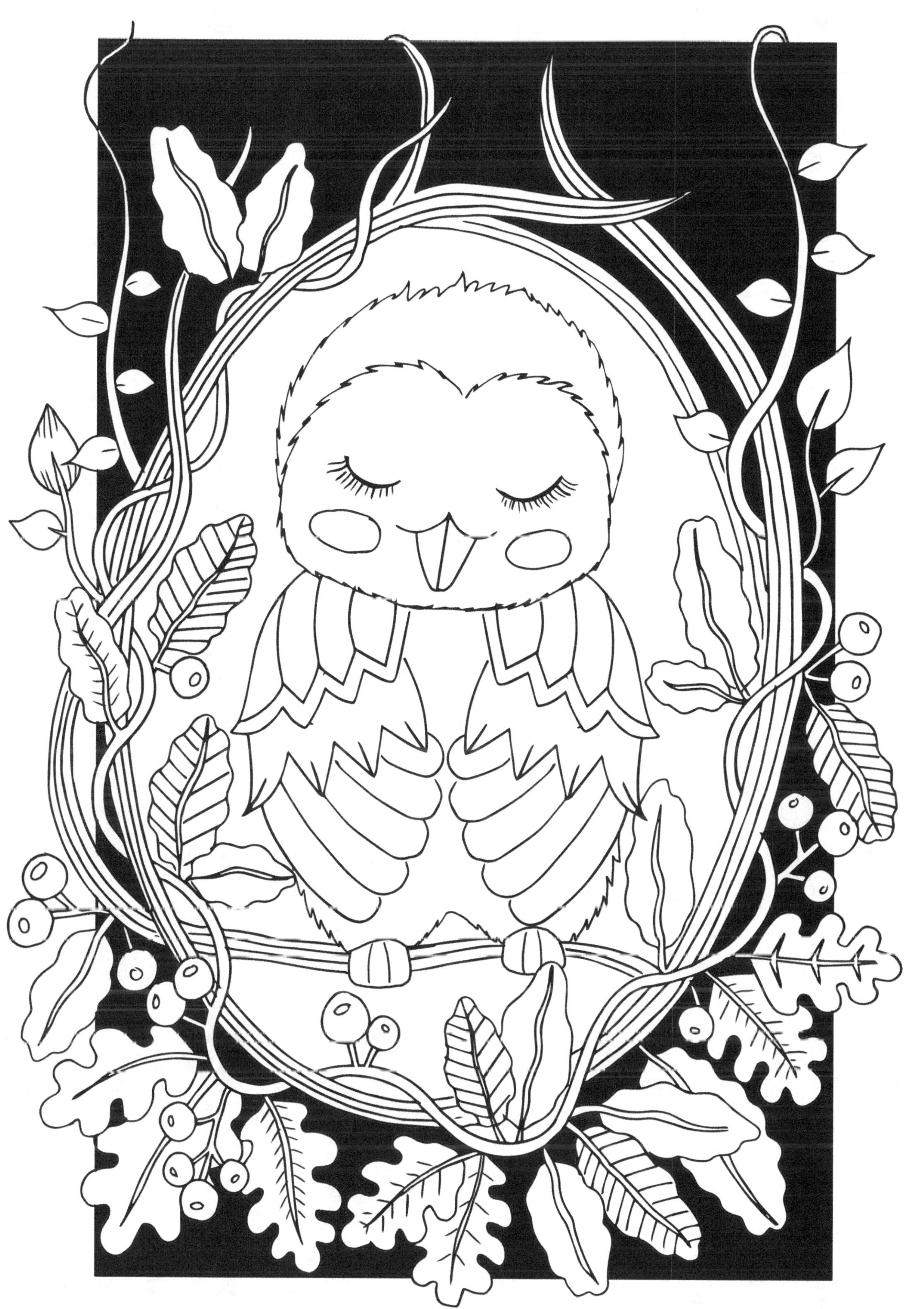

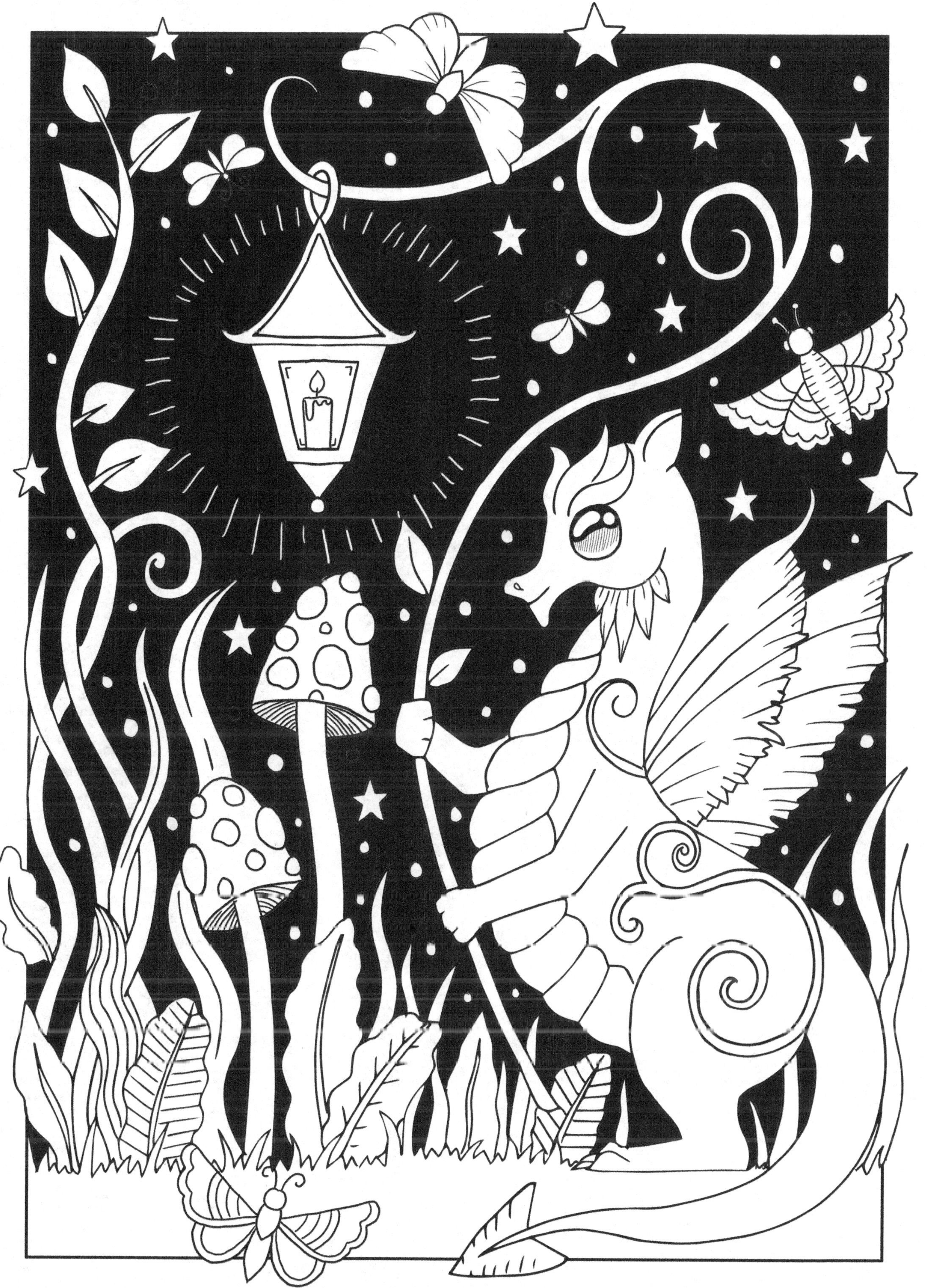

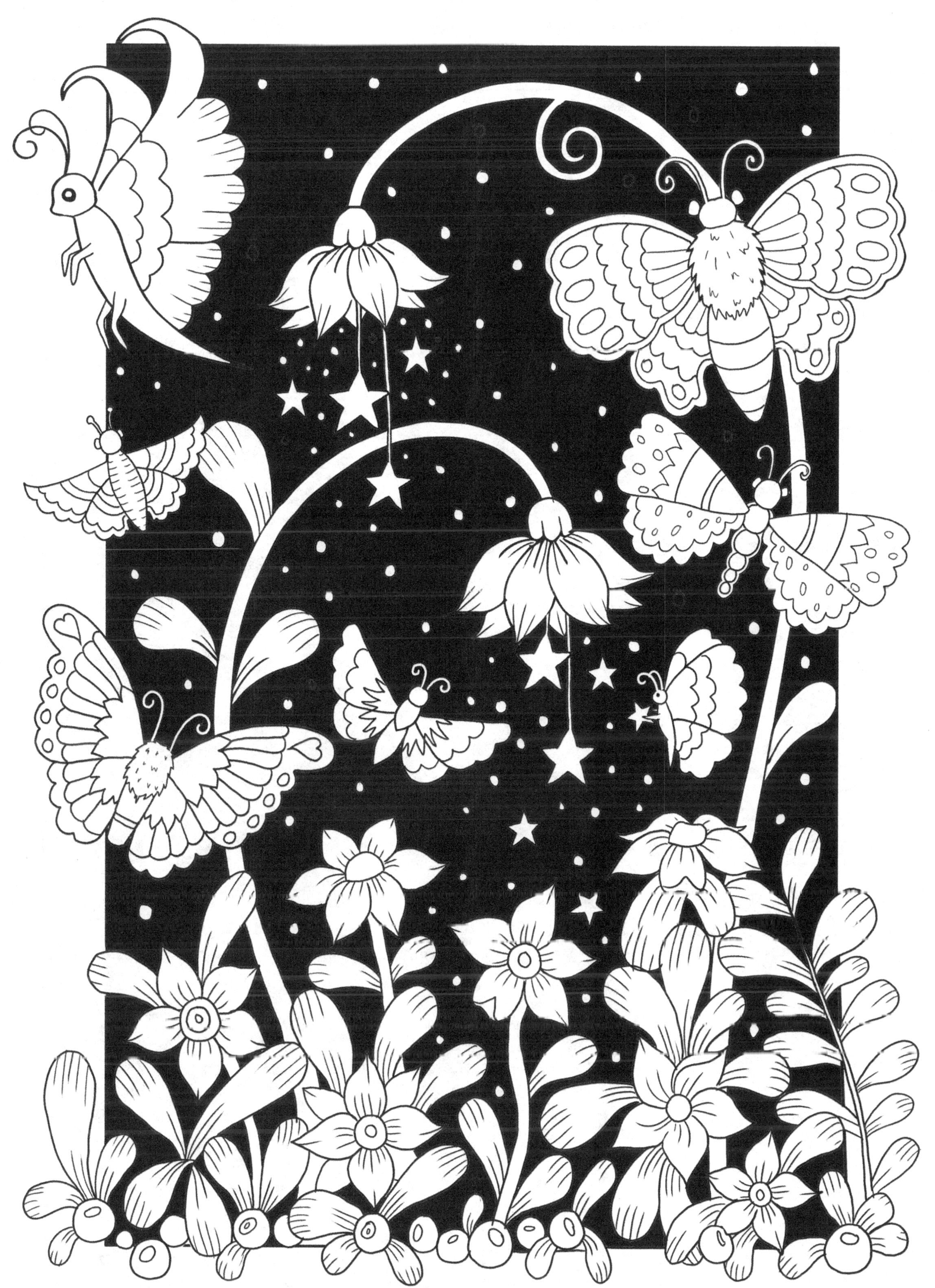

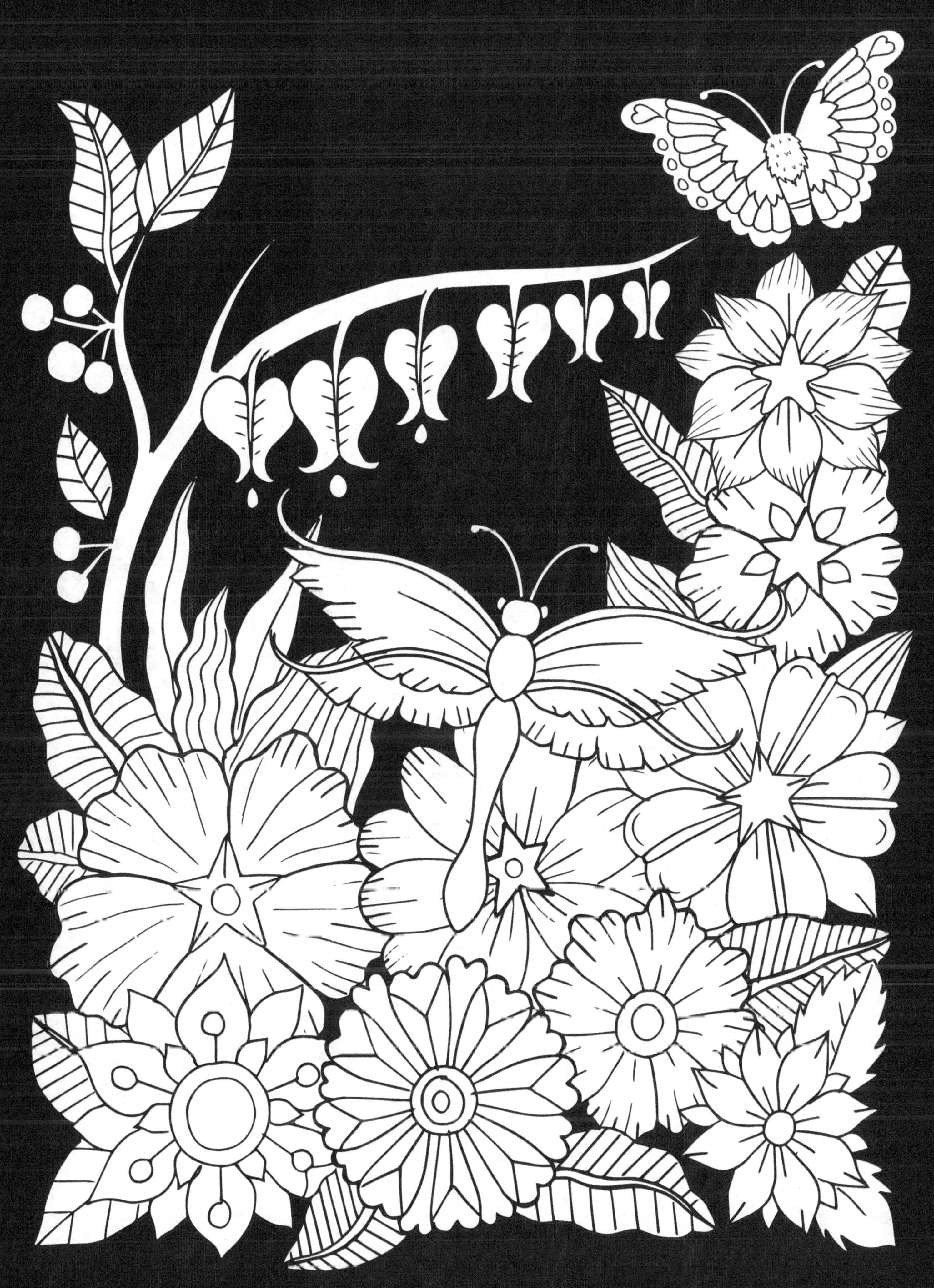

COLOR TEST PAGE

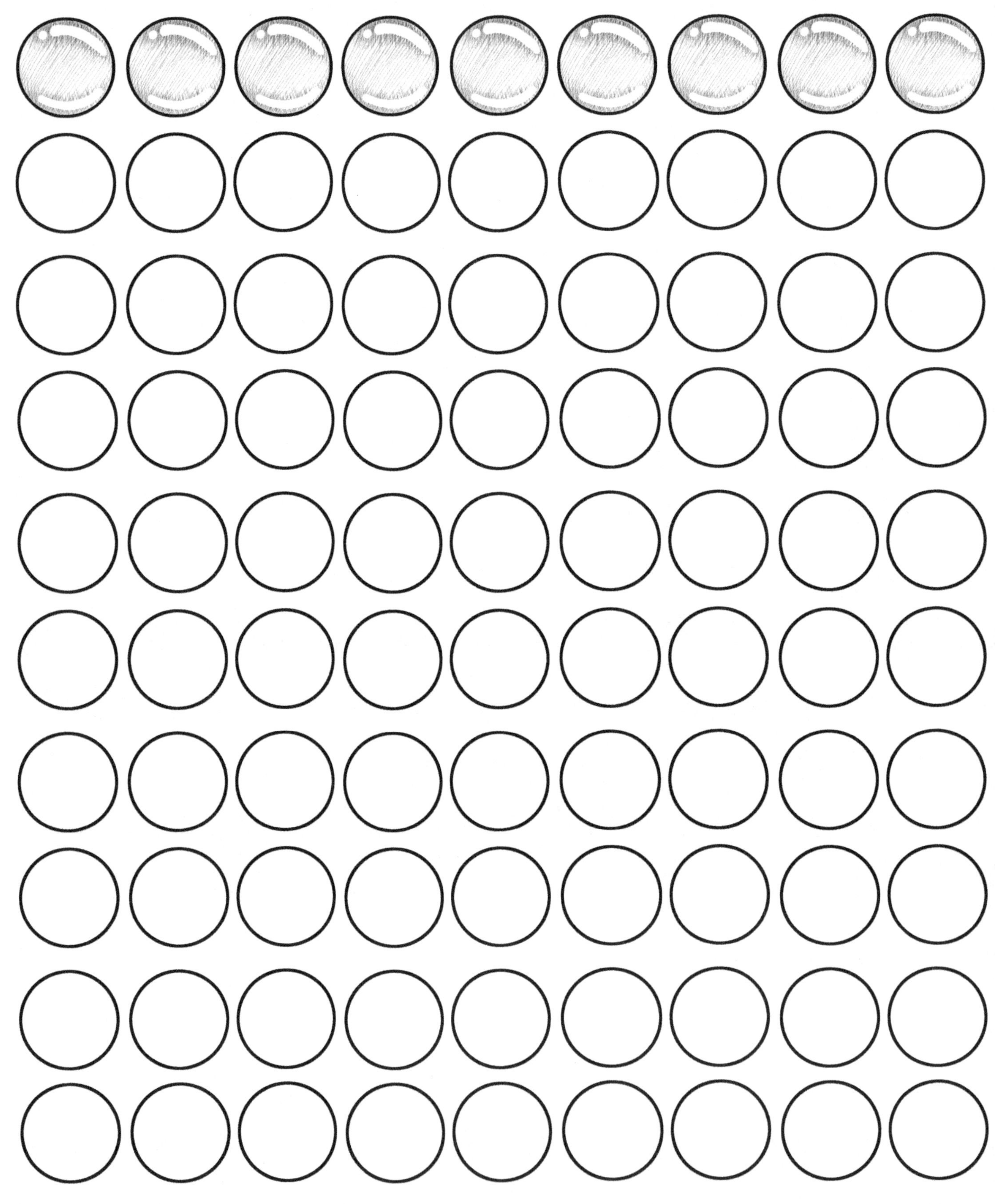

COLOR TEST PAGE

Made in the USA
Monee, IL
15 February 2026

44235220R00066